MASTER PLANNING

The Art of Exiting Your Business

HAWLEY MACLEAN
AND DAN SPRINGER

Hawley MacLean and Dan Springer -- 1st ed.

ISBN: 978-1-954757-60-8

The Publisher has strived to be as accurate and complete as possible in the creation of this book.

This book is not intended for use as a legal, business, accounting, or financial advice source. All readers are advised to seek the services of competent professionals in legal, business, accounting, and finance fields.

Like anything else in life, there are no guarantees of income or results in practical advice books. Readers are cautioned to rely on their judgment about their individual circumstances to act accordingly.

While all attempts have been made to verify the information provided in this publication, the Publisher assumes no responsibility for errors, omissions, or contrary interpretations of the subject matter herein. Any perceived slights of specific persons, peoples, or organizations are unintentional.

"To my parents, grandparents, great-grandparents, and the many generations of entrepreneurial family members that came before us whose dedication and vision helped build and shape our nation."

- HAWLEY MACLEAN

EXECUTIVE SUMMARY

Master Planning: The Art of Exiting Your Business is a comprehensive guide for business owners seeking to plan and execute a successful and fulfilling exit from their business. Authors Hawley MacLean and Dan Springer draw on decades of experience to deliver a strategic, emotionally intelligent, and highly actionable approach to transitioning out of ownership, with the goal of minimizing regret and maximizing both financial and personal outcomes.

Core Themes and Concepts:

1. **The Emotional Reality of Exit:**

    ○ According to the Exit Planning Institute, 76% of business owners experience regret within a year of selling.

    ○ A successful exit plan must consider not only finances but also emotional readiness, identity, and post-exit purpose.

2. **Proactive, Not Reactive Planning:**

    ○ Business exits are inevitable due to the "Six Ds": death, divorce, disability, distress, disagreement, and decline in health.

○ Planning early and thoughtfully is crucial to avoid being forced into suboptimal outcomes.

3. **The Role of the Dream Team:**

○ Effective exit planning requires a coordinated team of advisors: CPA, financial planner, attorney, banker, and more.

○ A dedicated exit planner or quarterback is essential to align all stakeholders and maintain momentum.

4. **Personal Financial Planning:**

○ The business is often the owner's largest asset; understanding the "wealth gap" (difference between post-exit needs and expected proceeds) is crucial.

○ Comprehensive planning includes lifestyle goals, taxes, estate strategies, and income needs.

5. **Contingency and Continuity Planning:**

○ Unforeseen events can derail a business quickly.

○ Owners must document plans and designate successors to ensure business continuity in their absence.

6. **Value Benchmarking and Acceleration:**

○ Most owners overestimate their business's value.

- True value is influenced by four intangible "capitals:" structural, human, customer, and social.

- Enhancing these areas—especially by reducing owner dependence—makes businesses more attractive and valuable.

7. **Strategic Exit Options:**

   - Exit routes include selling to family, employees, strategic buyers, or private equity; gifting or liquidating are other alternatives.

   - Each option comes with distinct financial, emotional, and tax consequences.

8. **Avoiding Common Pitfalls:**

   - Delayed planning, overreliance on gut feeling, poor documentation, and under-communication can severely hurt transition success.

CONTENTS

INTRODUCTION

Navigating through the multifaceted world of business ownership, you've undoubtedly confronted challenges and triumphs. I'm Hawley MacLean, and with over three and a half decades of experience and a heartfelt understanding of the realities of the entrepreneurial world, I extend a hand to help you through one of the most pivotal stages: transitioning out of your business.

What would determine a successful exit from your business? It's likely about obtaining that neat, efficient transition at a net value that meets or exceeds your expectations. It goes deeper, too. It's about steering smoothly into the next exciting chapter of your life, be it retirement, a new venture, philanthropy, or quality time with your loved ones, with enough financial resources to sustain your endeavors and dreams.

However, you might also wrestle with a silent adversary: regret. A staggering statistic from the Exit Planning Institute reveals that 76% of business owners encounter regret within a year of selling their businesses. It is essential that your exit strategy not only encompasses the financial and logistical facets but also makes your mental and emotional well-being a priority.

Overcoming Obstacles to a Smooth Transition

Successful exits can be hindered by procrastination, a lack of clarity on how to begin, or an absent team. Many owners find themselves deeply engrossed in operating their business, neglecting the crucial aspect of working on the business and preparing for its future in their absence.

Your exit is inevitable, and planning for it is not an option but a necessity. Your choices are concise: sell, gift, or liquidate. I've witnessed too many businesses vanish in the wind due to a lack of planning, especially when confronted with the "Six Ds:" death, divorce, disability, distress, disagreement, and decline in health.

A common issue I've identified among business owners is a lack of knowledge about the process of exiting a business. To many, their business is not merely an asset but their life's work. There's often a misconception about selling a business, thinking it's like selling an old car on Craigslist—post it and wait. But it's not that straightforward.

Shockingly, most business owners don't have a precise valuation of their businesses. Many base their desired sales price on their retirement needs, which, in reality, may not correlate with the actual worth of the business. This gap in understanding the actual value of their business versus what they believe it to be worth can lead to a tricky path of negotiations and potential disappointments.

Facing Fears

Business transition and exit planning may come with various emotions, apprehensions, and countless questions. Many clients express a fear stemming largely from the unknown and reluctantly addressing their or their business's mortality. A prevalent fear among them is losing their indispensable role or creative problem-solving ability in their business, especially when confronting prolonged sickness or disability. Imagine you are severely ill. How capable are you of solving problems or being creative? This perspective frequently goes unnoticed until it's glaringly obvious – usually in a time of crisis.

Here's another dimension that I often observe: the apprehension of not being needed anymore. Establishing a self-sustaining business that doesn't require your daily involvement can trigger a fear that you're no longer crucial to its operation. It's a psychological hurdle, but one that's surmountable with strategic planning and a clear understanding of your next chapter in life.

There is a matter of skepticism towards the exit planning process that often lurks in the minds of business owners. Rarely is there outright suspicion, but I've noticed a common thread of naive assumptions or underestimations about the process. Owners often think they can sell the business independently and devise ways to avoid taxes.

The IRS has seen it all when it comes to business sales, and well, trying to sidestep taxes or concoct some less-than-legal method of transferring or selling businesses will not end well. And while taxes and dealings with the IRS might make you wary, understand this: With a solid plan, you can significantly reduce or delay taxes. But doing nothing until the last minute guarantees the maximum tax output.

A pervasive thought among business owners tends to be, "Can I not manage this myself? After all, consultants just want to charge a fee."

You may think you and your CPA can handle it, and you might have a ballpark figure of your business's worth in your mind. But trust me, there's much more to it.

Remember, my aim as an exit planner is to have a meaningful, positive impact on your business, both now and in the future. With over 35 years of experience, my success hinges on the significant value I bring to my clients. We endeavor not just to be another team of advisors but to significantly enhance the process and success of your business transition, capitalizing on and amplifying the prowess of your existing team.

Hidden Enemies

Now, this is something many don't see coming: sometimes, our perceived "enemies" actually emanate from our inner circle or the advisors we've hired to guide us through this journey. Even well-intentioned family members can unknowingly become obstructions with contrasting views on how to proceed.

I've seen spouses locked in a power struggle — one yearning to safeguard every penny, the other eager to invest in the process to enhance the business's value and facilitate a successful transition. You'd think the common goal of prosperity would align them, but their differing views on how to reach that destination reveal friction we must acknowledge and address.

Don't forget competitors! Occasionally, fear looms that they'll catch wind of your succession plan, misconstruing it as an immediate selling of the business and sparking damaging rumors. Timing, too, wears the cloak of an enemy, convincing you it's either too early or too late to start the process. With a comprehensive planning process, we make timing irrelevant.

Your Questions, Answered

Numerous conversations and consultation sessions with clients like you involve questions that hold immense weight in shaping their exit journey. Perhaps these are lingering in your mind as well:

> *"What exactly is exit planning?"*
> *"What exit options are available to me?"*
> *"How much tax will I be required to pay upon exit?"*
> *"How much money will I need to exit my business?"*

In the following chapters, we'll answer these questions and more. We'll work on easing your fears and eliminating skepticism while we cover topics such as:

- Building your professional exit team
- Creating your personal financial plan
- Contingency and continuity planning
- Maximizing your business value
- Transition strategies
- Life after business

My experience in the business world, including owning, operating, and, indeed, exiting, grants me a unique perspective on your concerns. When I say, "We eat our own cooking," I envelop us in a shared experience. My team and I have navigated the paths of making payrolls, confronting competition, managing employee dynamics, and working through vendor and product issues. We have waded through the currents that can take your focus from working on your business to getting consumed by working in it, often clocking in exhaustive hours without dedicating adequate time to planning and strategy.

I've also spent substantial time immersing myself in exit planning, attending conferences, and engaging with professionals nationwide. Through these interactions, an observation has become abundantly clear: while skilled individuals are in the exit planning arena, many concentrate on isolated facets.

The MacLean team, however, brings something distinctive to the table - a comprehensive approach delivered by a group of independent professional advisors. We are dedicated to your business transition. We dig deep and wide, ensuring every possible outcome is thoroughly explored.

Many professionals don't give enough attention to whether or not you will have enough money to retire comfortably. Will you have enough to fuel your next business adventure or sail around the world? Enough to indulge in charitable pursuits or enjoy more moments with your children and grandchildren? The MacLean team looks at the sale *and* your life beyond it. My three plus decades in the field have reiterated the need for a process-driven approach when working with business owners. Big goals are achieved not by sporadic actions but through a diligently carved and adhered-to process.

The True Value of Success

When you think of success, what comes to mind? Is it a hefty bank account, or is it something a bit more intangible? You might find it surprising that in my years of doing this, a client has not defined their success by a specific dollar amount alone.

An instance that pops into my mind: I spoke to a client exploring avenues that could potentially channel an additional $500,000 into their pocket after all the taxes and transactions dust settled. Their response? "That'd be nice."

But that wasn't the end-all for them. What they placed above that half a million was ensuring their business lived on, that their customers remained in caring hands, that their employees retained a nurturing work environment, and that the deal was as beneficial for the buyer as it was for them.

So, what truly lights up the faces of those I help? It's gaining peace of mind, knowing where they're headed, how they'll get there, and what it'll all look like in the end. It's about continuity, stability, and a legacy that lives on beyond their leadership.

As you continue through the pages of this book, there's something I want you to take away: this isn't a "do-it-yourself" manual on how to exit your business. Exit planning is complex and intensely personal, and my intention here is to serve as your guide, providing a roadmap that steers you through the intricacies of exit planning. Our process-driven approach ensures you extract the utmost value and benefits from your business while enjoying a fulfilling, regret-free future.

- Hawley MacLean

CHAPTER ONE
Building the Dream Team

If you've been in business for a few years and have tasted success, you might think you've got your bases covered. You have your CPA, attorney, maybe an insurance advisor, and a few others in your corner. It sounds like a solid collection of professional advisors, but it's likely not operating as a true team. They're probably more like solo artists who rarely interact with each other. They work in their own silos, and you—the business owner—are left scrambling to bridge the communication gaps.

You're the one constantly reaching out, trying to stitch together their separate pieces of advice to solve the puzzle that is your business. Need a tax return? You go to your CPA. Facing a lawsuit? You call your attorney. It's reactive, and you initiate the conversation every single time.

A real team is a group of advisors who don't just wait for your call, but work collaboratively with you and each other. That's when you've hit the jackpot! Your existing advisors can morph into this dream team, but it requires a shift from being reactive to being proactive.

The Quarterback Approach

In any sport, without a good "quarterback" (aka team leader), the team falls apart. The same goes for your business. Exit planners are the quarterbacks for your advisory team. They ensure that everyone is moving in the same direction, that there's continuity, and that everyone is playing for the same win—increasing the value and profitability of your company and setting you up for a smooth exit, whether that's months or decades away.

You might be loyal to your current advisors, and that's commendable. Is there someone on your team that can fill the "quarterback" role? If not, finding an exit planning advisor can take that relationship to a new level and transform that loyalty into a powerhouse team that brings even more value to your business. Some advisors will grow with you, while others may no longer fit the bill. That's when you need to bring in fresh expertise to fill in the gaps.

Running a business can be lonely, but it doesn't have to be. Regular check-ins with your exit planning team are critical. They keep you from feeling isolated and overwhelmed by the weight of decision-making. Things are constantly changing, and as a business owner, you're perpetually busy. But that's exactly why you shouldn't have to bear the burden alone.

The Power of Synergy

You may have a blueprint in your mind for the future transition of your business, and you feel confident it'll succeed. But details get overlooked that can significantly affect the exit process. Is the structure of your business—the very entity of it—geared up to support this transition?

For example, we often find companies set up as C-Corps without a clear rationale. When all your advisors communicate, these historical decisions can be revisited to determine if they still serve your best interests—especially from a tax perspective as you prepare for a transition.

Your CPA's role should be more than just filing your taxes; they should take the lead from a financial standpoint on any strategic restructuring of your business entity to align with your exit. Meanwhile, your attorney weighs in on the legal structure and drafts agreements essential for the transition. Your value advisor's role is to pinpoint actions you should take to ramp up your business's worth. A financial planner will work in conjunction with your CPA to calculate the tax implications of the transaction, all while ensuring key personnel are incentivized to stay the course. These professionals often come together from the start, but as the exit comes closer, an M&A Advisor can also be beneficial in adding their expertise to the mix. Your exit planning advisor ensures that all team members are communicating and working towards your goal of a smooth and profitable exit.

Here is an example where the opinions of two experts on the value of a business differed. The business owner had received an opinion of value from their accounting firm for $4-$4.5 million, and the owner was prepared to run with this value. After taking the exit planner's advice and receiving a calculated valuation from a business valuation expert, the estimated value was revised to $3 million, indicating that there was work to be done on the business before going to market.

Here's another instance. A client was content with a sale price but faced a risky unsecured note stretched over five years. As a team, we dissected the terms and negotiated, resulting in secured interest on the loan and better collateral to mitigate the seller's risk.

Team synergy and regular, open communication can transform a good exit plan into a great one.

Navigating Team Dynamics

The path isn't always smooth when creating a dream team for your business exit. A common hurdle is dealing with advisors who are territorial or possess a big ego. These traits can lead to poor communication and hinder the collaborative effort required for a successful transition.

In the fast-paced environment of business transactions, responsiveness is key. There's a lot of "hurry up and wait," but when the time to act arrives, you need a team that can communicate efficiently and take swift action.

Expertise Versus Experience

Many advisors excel in their day-to-day operations but may lack experience selling or purchasing a business. When presented with new strategies, especially those involving tax deferral or complex legal structures, an advisor's unfamiliarity could result in an automatic—and perhaps unwarranted—dismissal of a sound idea.

You should seek out open-minded advisors who are willing to learn about new concepts rather than shooting them down due to a lack of knowledge. A knee-jerk negative reaction is a red flag; you want team members who are curious and collaborative.

The Cost of Ineffective Teamwork

Ineffective teamwork can lead to economic waste on an astronomical scale—it's estimated to be over a trillion dollars annually. The old adage holds true, especially here: there is no "I" in team. Advisors used to being the sole decision-maker might struggle to integrate into a group where their ideas aren't the only ones considered. You need advisors who are experts in their field and team players.

The Proactive Approach

Tony Gordon, a notable figure in the field, once said that after working with an accountant and doing battle all year, it often felt like counting the dead and bandaging the wounded when the CPA came in to clean up the mess at the end of the year. Instead, work with proactive advisors reaching out to you with their expertise, not just reacting after the fact.

Choose advisors with a proven track record, strong ethics, and a reputation for being tried and true. These types of advisors have been in the trenches for years and are not interested in suggesting anything that hasn't been thoroughly vetted.

The Financial Advisor as the Exit Planner

The financial advisor should know your situation best. 2024 Survey results by the Exit Planning Institute place the financial planner as the most trusted advisor. We believe this holds true, as a comprehensive financial planner truly has the BIG picture and is best suited for the quarterback role. The exit planner "quarterback" acts as the strategic coach, leading the team, calling the plays, and keeping every member aligned with the end goal. The benefits of working with the exit planner include:

- **Identifying Gaps:** Every business has gaps—discrepancies between where it is and where it needs to be. Among the most important is the wealth gap. Surprisingly, many business owners work tirelessly without a clear idea of their business's worth, the money needed post-exit or the impending tax implications. Coaches aim to quantify these elements because what you can measure, you can manage. Through a comprehensive financial planning process, you can expect a real world depiction of your entire financial future.

- **Managing Risks:** We'll discuss this more in a future chapter, but what happens when you become sick or injured and can no longer work as of tomorrow? You won't have five years to come up with a transition plan. Proper exit planning can help you manage this unexpected event and get the team on board to revise and execute an expedited plan.

- **Offering Expertise:** The MacLean Team has over 70 years of combined experience as financial advisors, witnessing countless transactions. Since most business owners we work with are navigating their first and only business sale, having someone who has seen what works and what doesn't brings extraordinary value. We are the center of the advisory network, interacting with all other members. We are inherently positioned to be the quarterback we mentioned at the top of the chapter because we are consistently reaching out, filling gaps, and identifying missing pieces in your financial plan.

- **Managing The Team:** The tale is all too common: a deal is signed, and only then does the business owner consult their CPA, resulting in reactive tax planning and often the highest tax rate possible. Involving a banking officer early on to discuss potential financing for the buyer is a proactive step to prevent deals from stalling. Similarly, having litigation attorneys review agreements before they're signed ensures they are defensible and enforceable.

Again, proper exit planning emphasizes proactive collaboration to avoid such scenarios. Your financial planner and your CPA are inherently pre-positioned to be the core of your exit planning team.

Additionally:

- **Understanding Buyer Types:** The type of buyer greatly influences the financing strategy for your business exit.

- **Strategic and Large-Value Buyers:** Strategic buyers and those making large-value purchases usually have their financing sorted out or may not require financing at all. They're ready to buy outright, which simplifies the transaction.

- **Small-Value Buyers and Internal Transfers:** Small-value buyers, employees, or family members will likely need financing. Here, a banker determines whether financing would come from you, the business owner, or a banking institution.

- **Helping Avoid Regrets and Remorse:** It's a sobering statistic that close to 70% of business owners experience regret or remorse after selling their business, primarily because they didn't receive the payout they expected or spent time exploring their post-sale lifestyle. Proper exit planning aligns the value you anticipate with future lifestyle and family goals.

The CPA

The CPA plays a critical role in minimizing the tax burden of a business transaction or deferring taxes to a later date. They also manage essential functions, including tax preparation, forensic accounting, and auditing. Let's look at some scenarios from a couple of our partner CPA firms:

"As part of a value growth and business transition strategies practice at a large regional CPA firm, we frequently partnered with clients to guide them through the planning process. We took a holistic approach, starting by understanding the owners' personal, financial, and business goals, both short- and long-term.

One standout case involved a small manufacturing business owned by two entrepreneurs in their thirties. Their vision was to retire well before the typical retirement age. We collaborated with their wealth advisor to model what achieving that would look like. The financial planning insights helped us establish specific goals for revenue, profitability, and overall business value.

With these goals as a foundation, we led a strategic planning process involving both ownership and their leadership team. The company committed to their plan and, over time, revised and improved it. Now, more than a decade later and two strategic planning cycles in, they've grown to nearly four times their original size. The owners still run the company, and thanks to sustained profitability and significant value growth, they are well-positioned to exit on their terms and retire early."

— Martha L. Sullivan, President,
   Provenance Hill Consulting, LLC

Another compelling example comes from Rick Krebs, CPA—also known as the "M&A Cowboy" and co-founder of the first Exit Planning Institute (EPI) Utah Chapter.

"I can't guarantee outcomes like this every time, but this is one of the best results we've seen. We worked with a SaaS company whose two partners initially targeted a sale price between $12 million and $14 million. After conducting a valuation, we

arrived at a closer estimate of $7–8 million. Fortunately, we had time—about 12 months—to work on increasing the company's value before going to market.

We brought in a value acceleration specialist and implemented two major changes: we fully developed their sales channels and helped groom an internal successor to become the CEO, allowing the current CEO to step down. We also cleaned up partnership structures and other financial elements.

After a year of work, they received multiple competitive offers. We ran a structured bid process, combining our buyer list with their inbound inquiries. Ultimately, they sold the business for $18 million—more than $10 million above the initial valuation.

This is the power of strategic exit planning. I'm not saying every case ends with a $10 million boost—but even a $2 million increase can dramatically improve the final decades of someone's life. A strong exit plan can mean the difference between financial freedom and financial strain in retirement.

Another example: I worked with a roofing company that initially went to market too soon. We call that 'business puberty'— the company still had some growing up to do. They weren't ready and got beaten up in the market. We regrouped, worked on value drivers for two years, and went back out. The result? Offers came in $2.6 million higher than before.

> *The takeaway is this: assembling the right team and starting early makes all the difference. Exit planning is not just a process—it's the single most effective way to increase the value of a business."*
>
> — Rick Krebs, CPA

Estate and Corporate Attorneys

Think of estate and corporate attorneys as the "fortress builders" assigned to protect your personal assets. These legal experts safeguard your wealth—now and for the future.

Trusts are a strategy used by attorneys to protect your assets. Trusts can be a game-changer in a substantial business sale. They have the potential to reduce your current tax burden while also minimizing the estate taxes that your heirs may face.

The Banker

With over 35 years as a co-founder and Director of a bank, I've learned that the right banker can make or break your exit plan. I always say, "It's impossible to do a good deal with bad people." So, make sure you choose a bank willing to work with you.

Local community banks offer flexibility and creativity that large national banks often can't match. For smaller transactions, where big banks demand conformity to rigid criteria, a community bank can be more accommodating to your unique needs.

One of my favorite questions to ask business owners is "Who's your banker?" instead of "What's your bank?" Your banker should know your business inside out and can act as a financial advisor, not just a lender. A good business banker will help you assess how a potential sale could be financed. They might not provide a valuation, but they can give you an idea of whether the proposed sale price is realistic based on your business's financial history and prospects.

The Compensation Plan Specialist

A compensation plan specialist ensures compensation structures are fair and equitable. A common misconception among employees is that ownership is the ultimate reward. But with ownership comes responsibilities like increased tax liabilities and the risk of litigation. Control, on the other hand, can be the real prize. It's about influence over decision-making and profits, not just having a stake.

After considering the liabilities, many employees realize they truly seek recognition for their contribution to the company's growth—a share in the increased value they helped to create. Incentive-based compensation plans can satisfy employees' desires to be rewarded for improving a company's value without burdening them with the drawbacks of ownership. These plans can be crafted to provide benefits from a sale, avoiding potential complications from minority interests.

Aligning Compensation with Company Goals

Incentive compensation plans should do more than supplement retirement plans like a 401(k); they should actively encourage behaviors that increase the company's value. This requires a tailored approach that resonates with the unique culture and goals of the business.

During the exit process, we often talk about "golden handcuffs" and "golden parachutes." Golden handcuffs are designed to retain key employees during and after the transition, ensuring continuity and stability. Golden parachutes offer a safety net for employees not retained by the new owners, providing a generous severance.

The Challenge of Perceived Entitlement

The hardest part is designing a plan that is both meaningful and motivating. Employees have grown accustomed to expecting bonuses as a part of participation, not necessarily tied to value creation. The challenge lies in crafting a compensation structure that aligns with long-term goals and recognizes actual contribution, not just presence, which is why the skill of a compensation plan specialist is so important in creating a transition that is as beneficial for the employees as it is for the owner.

The Business Attorney

The business attorney explicitly defines future adjustments to price, inventory, accounts receivable, or operating cash to protect your interests. They are instrumental in securing the intangible aspects of your enterprise, often referred to as the four C's: customer capital, social capital, human capital, and structural capital. These elements will be discussed in more depth later in this book. Though not always tangible, they are the foundation of your company's value.

Business attorneys often act as connectors to other legal specialists. They recognize when an issue requires alternative expertise and will guide you to the appropriate legal field, creating a comprehensive legal team that addresses all aspects of your business's value.

Don't Fly Solo

When the time comes to exit your business, it can be tempting to go at it alone. But here's our number one piece of advice: Don't! From the get-go, the focus should be on who is on your team and what skills and knowledge they bring to the table.

Our first conversation will revolve around your current advisory team. Who are they? What roles do they play? What is missing? It's like assembling a puzzle; we must identify the missing pieces to complete the picture. This becomes the basis of our entire process.

Approach the construction of your team with an open mind. Each member should have experience and knowledge, be a team player, communicate well, be responsive, and be willing to work with other advisors to get you the best deal possible.

KEY TAKEAWAYS

- Building a cohesive advisory team is essential; rather than a group of individual experts, a true team collaborates proactively for the business's benefit, aligning with the owner's goals.

- The role of an exit planner is like a quarterback, coordinating the team of advisors to ensure a unified approach to increasing business value and preparing for a smooth exit, whether soon or in the future.

- Open communication and regular meetings among advisors are crucial to avoid isolation in decision-making and to foster a dynamic where synergy can transform a good exit plan into a great one.

- Transitioning from a reactive to a proactive advisory approach can eliminate post-exit regret, ensuring that the value realized matches the owner's expectations.

- Each advisor, whether a CPA, attorney, banker, or compensation specialist, plays a unique and integral role in the process, and their collaboration is key to a successful business exit strategy.

CHAPTER TWO
Charting the Course:
The Personal Financial Plan

As a business owner, your enterprise is likely your most significant asset. A startling statistic reveals that about 70% of business owners regret selling their business within a year. Often, it's because the final proceeds from the sale didn't align with their expectations or needs to sustain their lifestyle post-exit. That's why having a well-thought-out, well-drafted, and well-executed financial plan is so important.

The Wealth Gap

A former client was already discussing selling his business and had even talked numbers. But when we assessed his financial needs - what we refer to as the "wealth gap" - it became clear that the offer he was considering was $250,000 short of what he needed to maintain his standard of living.

This client chose to proceed with the sale, fully aware that within a decade, they'd need to liquidate other assets to sustain their lifestyle. It was a deliberate choice, influenced by their desire for a particular buyer to acquire their business. But the key takeaway here is knowledge. Had they understood their wealth gap sooner, they might have approached the sale differently, perhaps even starting with a higher asking price.

Many business owners make a major mistake by basing their business's sale price on their financial needs. There's no direct correlation between what you need for retirement and your business's market value.

Setting the Foundation for Your Financial Journey

When you first meet with us, we strive to understand the full spectrum of your finances. Many professionals in this field focus narrowly on their specialty, whether it's investments, insurance, or legal documents. This narrow focus, unfortunately, dilutes the essence of what a proper financial plan should be.

We don't like the term "financial plan" since it is thrown around the industry generically. Our approach to financial planning is comprehensive. We look at everything - taxes, wills, trusts, health, lifestyle, goals, and travel plans. A great portfolio means little if it's eroded by taxes or conflicts with your life goals.

Our initial "first-time appointment" meeting is a high-level introduction to learn about your business, your aspirations, what's working for you, and what isn't. It's also an opportunity for you to learn about us - our process, our resources, and our credentials. The sole objective of this first meeting is to determine if there's a mutual fit. In this initial encounter, we're not here to sell you products or services. Instead, we're exploring whether our expertise matches with your needs and goals.

We understand that business owners may have questions about the cost or nature of our services. Our primary tools are not products but strategies and insights. We aim to give you peace of mind, clarity on your current position, a vision for your future, and a clear path to get there. If we all feel a connection and a potential for a beneficial relationship, we proceed to our "engagement meeting."

The Engagement Meeting

The journey from the initial appointment to the engagement meeting starts with our unique preparedness survey. This online survey, taking about 10 to 15 minutes, offers the business owner and us a clear numeric score on readiness to transition the business. When we discuss the survey results, this is often the first time a business owner sees a quantifiable score related to their transition preparedness. The survey breaks down into four categories, each providing insight into readiness. We then introduce the details of our "Master Planning Program." This program covers 12 categories over a year, each focused on adding value to your business transition process.

After gathering high-level goals and concerns in the first meeting, we define these more concretely in the engagement meeting.

Questions about when to sell the business and what comes next – whether it's starting another business or retirement – are addressed in detail.

Our wealth planning philosophy balances fixed expenses (like mortgages and insurance) with variable expenses (like travel and entertainment). We also consider your guaranteed income sources, like social security or pensions, and how these align with your expenses. Our goal is to cover your fixed expenses with guaranteed income sources and match up your variable expenses with variable assets, like your investment portfolio. This approach gives a holistic view of your financial plan.

In the engagement meeting, we provide a range of fees based on our discussions and the insights we've gained. Transparency at this stage is key to building trust and ensuring you're comfortable moving forward. The engagement meeting is a turning point where business owners decide whether to proceed with us.

The Fact-Finding Meeting

Our fact-finding meeting kicks off with what we internally refer to as the "shopping list." This is an extensive list of documents and information we need to start crafting your personalized financial plan. It typically includes three to five years of business and personal tax returns, financial statements, wills, trusts, insurance policies, investment details, and employee benefit packages.

How you organize and present these documents gives us an insight into how prepared you are. More often than not, business owners have their information scattered – with bookkeepers, bankers, attorneys, etc. This scattered approach signals that a big part of our role will be helping you organize your financial life.

The biggest challenge at this stage is gathering all the necessary information comprehensively and orderly. We understand this can be time-consuming and encourage business owners to take their time. The more thorough and complete the information provided, the more effective the resulting financial plan will be.

Once we have your information, we input it into our planning platform, creating a secure, personalized website. The website includes a digital vault where all your important documents are stored and accessed easily. The website regularly updates your financial information, providing an accurate and up-to-date picture.

At this stage, we can quote a firm fee, typically project-based, ensuring there are no surprises down the line. Communication is vital, and we encourage open dialogue without the fear of incurring additional costs. We also collect an onboarding or registration fee to cover the initial stages of gathering, organizing, and analyzing your data. We then choose a start date that works with your schedule and ours. Depending on your personal and business commitments, this could be immediate or a few months down the line.

In the fact-finding meeting, we focus on gathering data. Both spouses or partners don't have to be present – just whoever is most familiar with the financial details. This is a data-driven stage, setting the groundwork for the planning process.

The Planning Meeting: Aligning Facts with Goals

A few weeks after our fact-finding meeting, we come together again for the planning meeting. By now, we've thoroughly analyzed your financial data and understand your assets, liabilities, investments, and other financial elements. We start by reviewing a balance sheet we've created for you and have a detailed discussion of each asset and liability: investments, real estate holdings, insurance policies, legal documents like wills and trusts, and more.

As the business owner, your involvement in this meeting is highly valued. We explore the reasoning behind your financial choices — why you chose certain investments, the purpose behind your life insurance policies, and your objectives for each financial decision. We get into the details of your estate planning documents, like your will and trust, to understand your intentions. It's common to find discrepancies between what you believe these documents accomplish and what they actually do.

For example, one of our clients wanted to leave $5,000 to the person caring for their dog. After carefully reading through their will and trust, *everything* went to the dog's caretaker, and the rest of the family was left with the $5,000 to distribute amongst themselves. That was a significant "oops," so reviewing these documents is important to determine if they accurately reflect your wishes.

The Strategy Meeting: A Recipe for Success

As we enter the strategy meeting, we present all the options and tools necessary to achieve your objectives. We rarely offer just one solution; instead, we typically provide multiple options, each with pros and cons. Many clients seek a "silver bullet" or single solution to solve all their financial planning needs. However, effective financial planning is rarely about one big move. It's more often a combination of many smaller, well-coordinated steps.

We often compare financial planning to cooking. You can have the best ingredients, but the result won't be satisfying without a good recipe. And average ingredients can produce a fantastic meal with the right recipe. Similarly, financial planning combines investments, insurance, and tax strategies to create a successful outcome.

Business owners, like anyone, can have strong feelings about specific financial instruments or strategies. Some might dislike particular investment types, while others might prefer them. Our job is to build a balanced financial plan, considering these preferences and guiding you toward the most effective strategies for your goals. As your advisor, we present ideas and advice; ultimately, it's your plan. I'm open to your preferences and input. If there's something you don't like, we'll incorporate that feedback, always advising on the potential consequences or benefits.

Implementing and Reviewing the Financial Plan

After the strategy meeting, clients receive an executive summary and a detailed financial plan report. This documentation serves as a comprehensive overview of the options and strategies discussed. We allow clients time – a few days to weeks – to absorb and think about the plan, ensuring it fits with their expectations and comfort level.

Once the plan is reviewed and agreed, we reconvene to prioritize and schedule the implementation, deciding which aspects to enact first and setting a timeline for the remaining steps. In the early stages of implementation, frequent meetings are common – possibly two to three times a month- to ensure each part of the plan is effectively put into action and adjusted as needed.

After the initial intensive phase of your financial plan, we typically transition to quarterly meetings for the first year. Depending on the complexity and the number of moving parts in the plan, we may switch to semi-annual meetings later. The frequency is tailored to the client's needs and plan dynamics.

Our entire approach emphasizes the importance of preparation, clarity, and personalized strategies, creating a financial plan that is not just a document but a living blueprint that adapts and grows with you. As we guide you through this process, our commitment is to provide financial expertise *and* a partnership that supports and empowers you to make informed decisions, leading to a fulfilling and secure financial future.

KEY TAKEAWAYS

- Understand your "wealth gap" so the proceeds from your business sale support your post-exit lifestyle needs.

- A solid financial plan goes beyond investments and insurance; it encompasses taxes, estate planning, lifestyle goals, and even future travel plans, providing a holistic view of your financial health.

- The relationship between you and your financial advisor should be based on shared goals, trust, and a clear understanding of each other's roles and expectations.

- Preparedness for business transition is key; tools like the preparedness survey offer valuable insights into readiness and help form a tailored strategy for the business sale.

- Implementing a financial plan is a dynamic process that requires regular review and adjustment; it combines strategic steps rather than a one-time solution, ensuring ongoing alignment with changing needs and circumstances.

- Open communication and transparency in fees and processes are fundamental to building trust and maintaining comfort throughout the financial planning and implementation phases.

CHAPTER THREE
Preparing for the Unexpected: Contingency and Continuity Planning

W hen planning, you're most likely looking ahead five or ten years down the road toward retirement or selling your business. But you never know when something unexpected might happen. It's life's curveball, and it waits for no one.

Several years back, we had a client who owned a painting contracting company. We were working on a comprehensive plan, starting with his will and trust and getting him life insurance. The insurance came in a bit higher than expected because he was a smoker, something he hadn't disclosed. He decided to think over the higher premium, but went ahead with the policy and held off on the will and trust. Just two hours after leaving our office, he took a spontaneous flight on his plane. Tragically, he crashed and died. Just like that, everything changed.

Another client, an excellent skier, was out enjoying the slopes—a regular activity for him. Out of nowhere, a collision with another skier led to nine broken ribs, bruised organs, and an extended stay in intensive care. He found himself at the mercy of an unpredictable accident. Another client was riding their bike, hit a hole in the road, crashed and died. A young couple up the street had three young boys. The mother went in for a simple outpatient procedure and died. Six months later, her husband was found dead in their house from a stroke. You just never know.

I'm telling you these stories because they highlight an important aspect of planning—contingency and continuity. It's easy to think about the long term, the eventual exit or retirement, but what about the immediate? What if something happens today, tomorrow, or next week? Contingency planning ensures that your standard of living and business continuity aren't left to chance if the worst happens. The goal is to maintain the life and the business you've worked hard to build.

Defining Business Continuity in Exit Planning

Business continuity is closely related to contingency. Continuity is what we expect to happen, the ideal path your business follows as you step away due to retirement or other planned changes. It's the smooth transition we all hope for.

While we talk about continuity as the ideal scenario, we can't overlook the importance of contingency—the backup plan. Contingency covers the "what ifs." What if something disrupts the planned course? What if there's an unexpected turn? Contingency is the response to unforeseen interruptions to keep the business thriving rather than simply surviving.

Often, I've seen people confuse the two. They believe they have a continuity plan, but in reality, it's more of a contingency plan, a response to unexpected events rather than a well-thought-out strategy for planned changes.

The Core Five Ds

Every business owner must know the Five Ds: death, divorce, disability, distress, and disagreement. Each represents a life event or business situation that could dramatically impact your exit strategy.

While many are familiar with the Five Ds, we introduce a sixth: decline in health. This aspect is often overlooked but is just as impactful as the others. Including this makes us look at the broader picture of what might disrupt an exit plan.

We frame these Six Ds around the Exit Planning Institute's statistic that 50% of business exits won't be on the owner's terms, primarily due to one of these reasons. It's a sobering reminder of the unpredictability of life and business. It's not just about the dramatic "death scenario." More often, disagreements, the slow decline of health, or the creeping distress affect the business. If you have yet to de-risk through continuity or contingency planning, you're leaving the door open to fall into that 50% statistic of unplanned exits.

Common Pitfalls in Continuity Planning

Awareness of some typical stumbling blocks for business owners can help avoid consequences on your business's ability to navigate future uncertainties and transitions.

Procrastination

Procrastination is a universal trait, and business owners are no exception. Talking about the future, especially the "Six Ds" of exit planning, is uncomfortable. Often, you might find yourself or others in denial about family dynamics or business ownership issues, hoping they'll resolve themselves. This leads to kicking the can down the road, usually until it's too late and many planning opportunities have vanished.

Lack of Documentation

When we meet clients, often nothing is documented. You might have an idea or have discussed life insurance needs, but these plans aren't integrated into a formal exit strategy. There's usually no clear plan for who will speak to employees, contact vendors, or maintain operations if something happens. Frequently, the responsibility undesirably falls on the spouse. But without documented policies and procedures, everything becomes more chaotic and uncertain.

Complexity and Overwhelm

Many believe the exit planning process is too complicated. And yes, it can be, especially if it's your first time tackling such a task without a solid support team. However, the task becomes much more manageable when you have a good team and leadership. The challenge is not just in planning but in implementation—ensuring that everyone understands their role and the plan is actionable.

Failure to Implement

Even if there's something that resembles a plan, often it's not fully implemented. Maybe it's all in your head, or you've discussed it casually with a few people, but the essential documents aren't finalized, and the key players are not fully briefed. An unimplemented plan is as good as no plan.

Disjointed and Conflicting Instructions

For those who've made the effort to coordinate a plan, often it's done in silos. The business owner tries to manage it all, leading to inconsistencies. The buy-sell agreement might conflict with the will and trust. The spouse, key employees, and other stakeholders are told different things. This disjointed approach can create more confusion and conflict at the crucial moment.

Aligning Owner Goals with Business Needs

For many business owners, the struggle begins post-exit. After years of investing 60 to 80 hours weekly into the business, even during holidays and weekends, the sudden void after selling can be jarring. Many haven't thought beyond the sale, envisioning more golf or leisure but not grasping the full impact of this life change.

Relationships with spouses who are now around full-time can become unexpectedly strained. Establishing personal goals is vital, as these goals provide motivation and a sense of purpose once the business is no longer the central focus.

The first step in aligning your personal goals with your business's needs is understanding your goals. It's your plan, and while we aren't mind readers, the more information you provide, the better we can tailor your plan. This means sharing not just financial data like taxes, budgets, income, and investments but also what matters most to you. Do you want to leave a legacy? And if so, what kind? Every business owner will leave a legacy, whether you define it or leave it to be defined by others.

Your legacy could range from being remembered as a good business that cared for its employees and family to establishing a foundation with broader ambitions. The exit planning process is an opportunity to contemplate the type of financial future you aim for and the legacy you want to leave, distinguishing between what you need to live and what you want from life post-exit. After years of dedication to your business, this is your chance to dream big and plan accordingly.

Owner-Centricity

Owner-centricity can be a business's downfall or a value detractor. It's essential to analyze how dependent the business is on you. Our "Owner-Centricity Analysis" scores your involvement from 0 to 100%. We examine various business areas—sales, marketing, HR, bookkeeping, and financials—to determine where you're making decisions, delegating, or merely approving. The goal is to reduce your daily involvement to less than 25%. This minimizes the business's dependency on you, freeing up time for personal goals and making the business more attractive for exit or transition.

Empowering the Next Generation

Allowing children to step up and take ownership can be motivating and eye-opening, particularly in family businesses. Often, owners don't realize the potential within their children until they are given the opportunity to lead. This motivates the owner and revitalizes the business with fresh energy and perspectives.

Transitioning roles within a family business is deeply intertwined with the family's psychology and history. Encouraging adult children to take more leadership roles and make decisions can significantly change the dynamics, often for the better. We've witnessed daughters and sons stepping up, even in traditionally male-dominated industries, bringing new life and direction to the business. For example, one of our clients in the mining industry had a daughter who was helping with internal roles like managing the books. She was headstrong and ambitious, and because of that, she moved into a sales role where the customers loved her. She is currently the VP of the company, challenging any preconceived notions about her success in a "man's world."

Determining whether a family member or employee has the right skill set for leadership is a common challenge. Sometimes, those who seem promising may not live up to expectations, while others might surprise you with their capabilities. The key is working closely with potential successors and having a structured transition plan to gradually assess and develop their readiness.

Putting the Right People in the Right Seats

Whether you choose a family member or another successor, a seamless leadership transition begins with placing the right butts in the right seats. This means understanding the specific skill sets required for the business to continue thriving post-transition and ensuring the best-suited individuals fill those roles. Sometimes, this involves changing or fine-tuning roles and responsibilities, especially if team members have become complacent. It also involves uncovering hidden talents or addressing job security issues where individuals may be reluctant to share their knowledge or processes.

Health Impacts of Delaying Exit Planning and Retirement

A common observation among business owners who delay exit planning or retirement is the significant impact of stress. While some stressors are visible, like financial strain, many effects of stress are not immediately apparent. Stress can come from various areas—emotional, spiritual, financial, and more—and it often accumulates silently, taking a toll on both physical and mental health. Even if you're eating well and exercising regularly, the underlying stress from running a business can still affect you in ways you might not immediately recognize.

Strategies for Managing Health While Running Businesses

❖ **Reduce Owner-Centricity**

If the business is less dependent on you, it naturally reduces the stress and pressure on you as an owner. Building a trusted team and delegating responsibilities can significantly alleviate the constant burden and allow mental and physical recuperation.

❖ **Focus on Fundamental Health Practices**

Regular exercise, maintaining a healthy weight, and avoiding harmful habits like smoking are all foundational to managing stress and improving overall health. Take time to step away from the business periodically, as these breaks allow for relaxation, re-energization, and perspective, which are essential for long-term health and business success.

Exit planning is a commitment to yourself, your family, and the legacy you wish to leave behind. We hope this chapter prompts you to start those conversations, document those plans, and take those steps toward a future where you and your business can thrive, regardless of life's unexpected turns.

KEY TAKEAWAYS

- Life's unpredictability necessitates contingency and continuity planning, ensuring that personal and business affairs can withstand unexpected events. Understanding and preparing for the "Six Ds," including the often-overlooked aspect of health decline, is crucial for exit planning.

- Procrastination and a lack of documentation are common pitfalls in planning. Move beyond mere intention, formalizing plans and keeping all stakeholders informed and involved.

- Aligning personal goals with business needs contributes to your post-exit fulfillment and well-being.

- Reducing owner-centricity by delegating responsibilities and empowering the next generation or suitable successors helps create a more resilient and attractive business for future transitions, reducing stress and improving your health.

- A well-crafted exit strategy is a commitment to personal health and the legacy one leaves behind.

CHAPTER FOUR
Knowing Your Worth: Value Benchmarking

I n our 35 years of experience in financial planning and banking, one truth stands out: most business owners, possibly including you, don't understand their business's value accurately. According to a 2022 study by Massachusetts Mutual Life Insurance Company & LRW, around 60% of owners tend to overestimate the worth of their businesses, while a significant remainder undervalue theirs.

Let's talk about where many of us get it wrong. There's a belief that valuing a business is straightforward, perhaps a simple multiplication of gross revenue or EBITDA. We've seen many people decide their business's price tag based on the sum they need to retire comfortably. This approach, while understandable, is flawed. The reality is that potential buyers are not swayed by how much money you need to retire. Instead, they're focused on the intrinsic value and potential return on their investment.

The valuation process varies significantly depending on who's interested in buying your business. From family members to key employees, small-value buyers to large ones, and strategic buyers, each has a different view of what your business is worth to them. For instance, a strategic buyer might be willing to pay a premium for your business because of its unique advantage to their existing operations.

The Valuation Journey

Navigating through the valuation process is more complex than slapping a price on your business. It involves a deep understanding of the market, the buyers, and the various factors contributing to a business's value. Whether it's for selling, securing a loan, or planning for the future, knowing the worth of your business serves multiple purposes. Banks, for example, may value your business conservatively when considering it as collateral for a loan. On the other hand, a strategic buyer looking for synergy might place a higher value on your business than any other type of buyer.

We encourage you to start thinking about valuation from a practical standpoint. If you were on the other side of the table, how much would you pay for your business? How long would it take to recoup that investment? This perspective can offer a grounding starting point for understanding valuation beyond numbers.

Valuation doesn't have to be an expensive, one-off exercise. There are cost-effective approaches like value benchmarking, which use national databases to provide a ballpark figure for planning purposes. This can be an excellent first step in your exit planning journey without committing to the full expense of a detailed valuation.

Beyond the Balance Sheet: Assessing Strategic Value

A company's true value extends well beyond its financial metrics. While traditional measures like revenue, EBITDA, and net income provide a snapshot of operational performance, they often fail to reflect intangible assets that can dramatically increase a business's market appeal and sale price. This is what Rick Krebs, CPA—known in the industry as the "M&A Cowboy"—refers to as *"thinking outside the books."*

According to Krebs, "Blue Sky" value—or goodwill—includes those elements that don't show up on the balance sheet but are critical to buyers. This might include brand recognition, exclusive sales channels, proprietary technology, or unique processes. These components create a competitive advantage that makes a company more desirable and, often, significantly more valuable.

In one example, Krebs shared that a SaaS company he advised had developed exclusive inroads with some of the world's most prestigious universities. These relationships weren't accounted for in the company's financial statements, yet they were a major reason strategic buyers were willing to pay a premium. As Krebs explains, *"These inroads and sales channels are what pushed that value up. They weren't reflected in the numbers, but they drove real, strategic worth."*

When preparing for an exit, Krebs emphasizes the importance of identifying and highlighting these key value drivers—especially intellectual property and human capital. *"What does your management team look like? Do you have strong leadership in place?"* he asks. These questions speak to the internal strength and scalability of a business—factors that don't always translate neatly into financial data but are deeply compelling to buyers.

Krebs also underscores that every business has a "secret sauce"—a distinct advantage that sets it apart. In one notable transaction, he facilitated the sale of a custom cabinet company that had perfected a proprietary process for building and finishing cabinetry. Their craftsmanship attracted elite clientele, including celebrities, with some kitchens selling for $200,000 to $400,000. Despite the exceptional quality and reputation, none of this value was visible in the financials. *"They weren't just Home Depot cabinets,"* Krebs explains. *"They were works of art, backed by 30 years of reputation and innovation."*

Krebs warns that if these intangible value drivers aren't identified and properly communicated, they can be easily overlooked, leading to significant undervaluation. However, strategic buyers—those who see the potential beyond the numbers—are often willing to pay a premium for them. *"When you hit certain thresholds on these value drivers, the selling price goes up not just linearly, but exponentially,"* he says.

Ultimately, as Krebs puts it, the goal is *"getting [buyers] to pay more for your business"* by uncovering and showcasing its full strategic value. By focusing on both tangible and intangible assets, sellers can better position themselves for a profitable exit and a more secure retirement.

—Based on insights from Rick Krebs, CPA
Co-founder, EPI Utah Chapter | "The M&A Cowboy"

Understanding and articulating the strategic value of your business—the intellectual property, unique processes, human capital, and reputation that make up your "secret sauce"—is only part of the equation. To truly prepare your business for a successful exit and maximize its value, you must take a holistic approach. Look beyond isolated value drivers and assess the foundation on which your business is built. This means emphasizing the importance of identifying and communicating what makes a company valuable outside of its financials.

Once those elements are identified, the next step is strengthening and aligning them within a broader framework. That's where the Four Pillars of Value come in: structural, human, customer, and social capital. These pillars provide a comprehensive lens through which to evaluate and enhance your business, ensuring it's not only profitable—but also scalable, transferable, and ultimately sellable.

The Four Pillars of Value

We guide business owners to look at their companies through a broader lens, identifying value across four areas as defined by the Exit Planning Institute: structural, human, customer, and social.

- **Structural Value:** Documented procedures and well-established systems make your business a plug-and-play opportunity for the new owner, significantly enhancing its appeal and value.

- **Human Value:** Maximizing value involves having the right people in the right seats. This might mean recognizing the hidden talents of long-standing employees or promoting from within to fill critical roles. Such moves enhance the operational efficiency of your business and strengthen its culture. A strong, cohesive team directly translates to improved performance and, by extension, increased business value.

- **Customer Value:** Your relationship with your customers, their loyalty, and the diversity of your client base are all factors that buyers will pay attention to. However, this area can also pose a unique set of challenges. The core issue lies in customer concentration—a high dependency on a limited number of customers for a substantial portion of your revenue. This dependency can significantly amplify the risk profile of your business. Imagine the impact of losing one or two of your top clients; if they represent half your revenue, the stability of your business could be jeopardized.

  The solution is diversification by broadening your customer base and service offerings. Don't just add new products or services haphazardly. Strategic expansion will make your business indispensable to your customers. By introducing complementary services or products, you create a more resilient revenue stream that is less vulnerable to competition and customer loss.

  A key to this process is understanding your ideal customer and why they chose you. Attempt to see your business through their eyes and align what's important to them with what's important to you. This exercise in empathy will solidify your customer relationships and clarify your value proposition to prospective buyers.

- **Social Value:** This refers to your business's reputation, brand strength, and presence in the community and market. A strong, positive brand image can significantly contribute to your business's perceived value. This is where strategic marketing and brand management come into play. A comprehensive marketing and brand assessment can uncover opportunities to strengthen your brand's presence and perception in the market. Remember, a potential buyer isn't just acquiring your financials; they're stepping into your brand's legacy. A tarnished reputation or weak brand positioning can lead to discounted offers or deter buyers altogether.

While you may be focused on the financial success of your business, potential deal breakers lurk beneath the surface regarding these four pillars of value. If your internal processes are chaotic, too much revenue depends on too few clients, or there needs to be better team cohesion, these issues will come to light during due diligence. Such revelations can not only diminish the perceived value of your business but could also derail potential deals entirely. Invest in and develop the aspects of your business that make it unique, resilient, and attractive to potential buyers.

Fine-Tuning Financials for Maximum Value

We often tell business owners that their financials and valuations can either be worth their weight in gold or act as a crippling liability. This holds true across the board, whether you're considering a strategic sale, a sale to employees, or even transitioning ownership within your family. How you've prepared your financials can significantly impact your ability to secure financing for the next phase of your business journey.

As business owners, many of us have performed the balancing act of combining legitimate business expenses with those that might "push the envelope." While optimizing your tax benefits is a smart business move, the real challenge emerges when presenting a clean, transparent financial picture to potential buyers or lenders. You must extract those personal or discretionary expenses to showcase your business's true profitability and operational efficiency.

Also, ensure that your financials are consistent with your tax returns and accurately reflect the business's performance over time. Present them in an organized manner to allow buyers to focus on the strengths and potential of your business rather than getting bogged down in financial ambiguities. Clarifying one-time events, reclassifying misallocated expenses, and providing detailed notes can contribute to a smoother due diligence process and a more favorable assessment of your business's value.

Enhancing Value Through Retirement Contributions

One strategy we've found particularly effective in bolstering a business's valuation is maximizing retirement plan contributions. This approach provides a clear, traceable path of discretionary cash flow and leverages tax advantages in a way that's both legitimate and beneficial to the business's value. For instance, every dollar contributed to a retirement plan could potentially increase the business's value by five times that amount, showcasing how strategic financial planning can significantly impact your valuation.

Accuracy and Timing Are Everything

Getting your valuation right is of the utmost importance. We once encountered a business owner who received two very different valuations—one from our team and another significantly higher from a large national accounting firm. This discrepancy led to an unrealistic asking price and a stalled deal. Even though it was a reputable national firm, they didn't know the client's business intimately and delivered a quick, high-level valuation. Their number was significantly overestimated.

In contrast, our business valuation expert took the time to understand the business and its financials in depth, arriving at a more realistic figure. Unfortunately, the owner chose to go with the higher number, assuming it would be accepted. It wasn't—and the deal fell through.

Undergoing a valuation process serves as a dress rehearsal for selling your business. It involves a third party scrutinizing your financials and comparing your business to others in the market, providing a realistic view of your company's value and preparing you for the questions and challenges potential buyers will present. Engaging in this process early allows you to defend your valuation with confidence, armed with the knowledge and insights gained from a thorough, impartial evaluation.

This is where mindset becomes critical. As Rick Krebs, CPA, says, *"I want to change their thinking and their approach from income generation to value creation. When we are looking at an exit, we are trying to change that to value creation."* That shift in thinking—from short-term profitability to long-term value building—is what separates those who exit successfully from those who struggle.

Don't wait to get a valuation. Starting early only benefits you, whether it's a benchmarking exercise, a calculated valuation, or a certified valuation. Valuation professionals use standardized data and methodologies, so differences in final numbers should be minimal. However, engaging in this process early gives you a comparative insight into how your business stacks up against others in your industry.

The goal of valuation and exit planning is not just to exit your business but to do so in a way that reflects its true value and ensures its legacy continues. By focusing on accurate valuation, understanding transferability, and preparing thoroughly, you're setting the stage for a successful transition that honors the hard work and dedication you've invested in your business.

KEY TAKEAWAYS

- Understanding the true value of your business requires more than simple financial metrics; it involves assessing strategic, structural, human, customer, and social aspects that contribute to its overall worth.

- Valuation is not a one-size-fits-all process; different buyers will value your business differently, with strategic buyers often willing to pay a premium for its unique advantages.

- Practical, cost-effective approaches like value benchmarking can provide a helpful starting point for exit planning without the full expense of a detailed valuation.

- The strategic value of a business, including elements like brand reputation, customer loyalty, and organizational structure, can significantly enhance its attractiveness to potential buyers.

- Early and accurate valuation, combined with strategic financial planning and a focus on maximizing the business's unique strengths, is essential for a successful exit that honors the business's legacy and ensures its continued success.

CHAPTER FIVE
Accelerating Your Business Value

We've yet to meet a business owner who has said, "Hey, my business is making too much money; let's dial it back a notch." Successful people are always looking for ways to boost profits, build equity, or find more time for the things that truly matter, like family or hobbies. Accelerating value means different things to different people. For some, it's all about stacking up those dollar bills and seeing the bottom line soar, and for others, achieving that elusive work-life balance or fostering a workplace culture that feels like family. All of those definitions are valid. Let's explore some areas of your business that can directly impact value regardless of your definition of value acceleration.

Overlooked Areas of Improvement

The Four Cs

Most business owners focus on tangible assets—cold, hard cash—instead of intangible assets, which you can't quite put a price tag on.

As discussed in Chapter Four, these are the 4 Cs: human capital, social capital, structural capital, and customer capital.

Human capital describes the people who keep our businesses running. And though business owners might know how each person is being utilized, we wonder if they spend enough time building those people up or assessing whether each person is in a position to use their skill set to the maximum potential. With every business we help, the conversation starts with, "Do you have the right people in the right roles?"

Social capital is how all of these different people relate. Do they act like a team? Do they communicate well? Do they support each other? For example, we worked with a business in the transportation industry, and the owner wanted to get out. He tried to step back and do less and thought his key person was someone who could do everything he could do. However, while the owner was spending time away from the business, the key person demonstrated a significant lack of ability in some critical areas. So, we had to make some decisions about training this person to improve or to replace them.

The owner decided to replace them with a new general manager. It was a disaster. The general manager had good people skills but no computer or financial skills. So, that person ended up leaving the company. We were back to building up by bringing in two other people who previously did some financial bookkeeping jobs into the key person role. We created more of a team between the key people by analyzing their strengths and weaknesses. It turns out that the original key person and the two other people in the business had *all* the skills necessary to allow the owner to feel comfortable about stepping back and letting the business run itself. Exploring team dynamics always reveals something people want to avoid discussing, even though it might have been known. You might realize that you already have the team you need once you open the doors of communication.

Regarding structural and customer capital, your customer lists, processes, and procedures hold substantial value. Remember that if most of your revenue comes from a small group of customers, it's a value killer. Even if your processes and procedures have never been scrutinized for efficiency or documented because everyone just "fell into place" operationally, there is always room to improve and document these processes floating around in your head.

Technology

Since the dawn of time, the model has been "the more money my business makes, the more valuable it is." But that model is changing. You could have a business that's making more money each year; however, the actual sale price of that business could be going down because of the impact of technology and competition. For example, let's say you wanted to sell your business for a few million dollars, including the building and inventory. A prospective buyer might say, "Well, why would I go ahead and buy this business for a few million dollars when I could start it myself and rely on technology more, replicating the business for half the cost?"

Over the next ten years, focusing on these overlooked areas of value acceleration will become more important as baby boomers sell their businesses. With more competition, this will put downward pressure on the sale of your business.

Identifying Areas of Improvement

How can business owners effectively pinpoint areas for improvement within their ventures? A risk assessment tool is a valuable resource for identifying potential areas of enhancement. However, the tool is only as good as the team of advisors you assemble, who should be well-versed in strategies for value enhancement. When you open up your toolbox, and all you have is a hammer, everything starts to look like a nail. This isn't a dig at other professionals. Each discipline brings its unique perspective to the table. Whether it's a CPA focusing on maximizing deductions, an attorney suggesting legal maneuvers, or an investment advisor advocating for stock and bond investments, each advisor brings their own lens to the equation. But there's rarely a one-size-fits-all solution. The key lies in crafting a tailored strategy encompassing a blend of approaches, whether fostering human capital, fortifying financial structures or tackling other facets of business operations.

Enhancing value takes a hands-on approach that can only be achieved by human interaction between yourself and a value advisor. You can't use a tool or AI to do this. Your value advisor will conduct team meetings to find out how everyone feels about their role and how they contribute to the company's overall success. Business owners know how to run businesses but often don't know how to manage people best. Not effectively managing people can be a real value killer. If you don't prioritize it, customers will feel it.

Let's look at an example that sheds light on our approach to identifying areas for improvement and paving the way for growth. We worked with an engineering firm planning a key person transfer, but the key person unexpectedly left. It was a family business with a husband, wife, and their two daughters. Even though both daughters worked there, the mom often excluded them from decision making and business learning opportunities. We felt it was simply because she didn't want to see her daughters fail, but she was holding them back from contributing to the company's growth. We were able to help the family dynamics in that situation by "ripping off the band-daid," so to speak, and allowing the children the chance to fail so they could learn from their mistakes. These learning opportunities have contributed positively to the value of the business.

Setting the Stage for Growth: A Culture of Unified Vision and Direction

Over the years, we've learned that every business has a culture. Even the most dysfunctional team has a culture—a culture of dysfunction. A positive culture is crucial to value acceleration. Any amount of toxicity that leaks into the positive culture you are trying to create will destroy value.

That is why it is essential to establish a unified vision and direction by gathering the key players in the company, including the owner and their spouse. We ask each person a series of questions to illuminate the path forward. Where do we stand as a company? Where do we aspire to be in the next three, five, or even ten years? Who will take us there, and how do we plan to get there? And perhaps most importantly, what's waiting for us at the finish line?

All of them typically have very different answers to each question. But, the goal is for us to come back after a year has passed, ask the same questions, and have everyone produce the *same* answers.

Can you imagine how powerful that would be for your business? Everyone should have a unified vision. What does it look like when you are doing your best work? Where do you see the company going? Alliances and alignment within the team should be evident when we ask these questions. This creates the foundation you can build on and start creating value. If you have two people who want to grow the company and spend all their time doing it and one who is complacent and satisfied with where the company is currently, these conflicting goals will not contribute to accelerated value.

Don't underestimate how much power your people have to maximize or crush value. We recently worked with an owner who was excited about the growth phase of their business, and then, suddenly, two key employees just up and left. It destroyed any trajectory of growth and value acceleration, as it took a year to get the right people in the right seats again and everyone working toward a common goal.

We have another client who took four years to get rid of a toxic employee because that person had been there for 20 years. The owner avoided the situation altogether because they thought it would become a nasty legal situation. But that person held them back from three years of growth. And finally, they're gone, everyone in the company is relieved, and they can regain their focus.

Creating a team of like-minded individuals with similar goals from the very beginning helps people excel in their positions and contribute to overall value. When deciding between two new hires, we often recommend using a retirement plan as a hiring tool. If one candidate is more attracted to the retirement plan, hire that one. This indicates their desire to have long, stable, and productive employment with you. These types of hires contribute to a team with a clear focus, communication, and a vision for growth, unlike a team of people who want to live paycheck to paycheck. As an owner, remember to include these valuable employees in decision-making processes and ask them periodically about their likes and dislikes about the company. They will feel grateful that their opinion matters, which will go a long way.

Value Acceleration Strategies

To determine what value acceleration strategies will work best for your business, we always start with a large funnel and narrow it down to a couple of best strategies. We always tell our clients we're horrible at reading minds, so the more insight you provide, the better your plan will be. The most important thing to remember is that it's *your* plan. A good value advisor will do frequent check-ins to ensure you are still comfortable with the chosen path, and adjustments can always be made.

When we discuss the 4 Cs, we quantify them with an estimated value you can expect from working on each area. We always choose the activities that add the greatest value. As the owner, you can decide if you have the time and energy to commit to increasing value before going to market or if you want to start the transition process immediately.

We consider all aspects of value acceleration, even some that may not be obvious. For example, we worked with a company with a good offer of about $7.5 million from a value-type buyer, but upon further consideration, we determined they might be very well positioned to sell to a strategic buyer. Within 90 days, they had a strategic buyer offering $14 million in all cash. Even though the company didn't have to change a thing internally, just a simple change in the type of buyer resulted in a significantly higher value.

Another company we worked with was rapidly expanding its retail stores over ten years, with almost 20 stores. However, they had major issues with staff and turnover. We had to make a strategic shift to focus on developing key people since the owner needed help handling the massive growth. He questioned why he hadn't stopped buying more stores five years prior. But in this instance, we had to stop the growth plan and work on structural capital to re-harness the potential for value acceleration.

Stay the Course

We often say, "If you can't measure it, how can you manage it?" To keep you motivated on the value acceleration journey, we start with a baseline number so that you can track your progress toward that number quarterly or yearly. Every business and culture is different, so the time needed to build value will vary depending on your circumstances. But even owners who sit down and say, "Gee, this is taking a long time, and I don't feel like I'm making any progress," are often pleasantly surprised to find out how much has been accomplished while they were in the trenches. Your value advisor will remind you of the actual, measurable steps that have been taken toward value growth. A milestone for any business owner is seeing the business becoming more self-sufficient and less dependent on them. This excitement is a primary driver of staying committed to the value acceleration process. When you get there, pat yourself on the back for staying the course.

KEY TAKEAWAYS

- Boosting business value goes beyond cash flow to enriching the Four Cs: human, social, structural, and customer capital.

- In a world where business dynamics are rapidly changing, leveraging technology can differentiate between a thriving business and one that merely survives.

- Utilizing a risk assessment tool and assembling a diverse advisory team is fundamental to pinpointing improvement areas. A blend of perspectives leads to a more robust value enhancement strategy.

- A unified team vision and a culture of support are non-negotiables for growth. When everyone is on the same page, the company's trajectory toward value acceleration becomes more apparent and achievable.

- Regular strategy reviews ensure your plan stays on target. Remaining flexible and responsive to change can lead to significant gains.

CHAPTER SIX
Paving Your Path: Transition Strategy

T he decision to sell your business requires understanding who you might sell it to and how that impacts its value. You can take three main paths with your business: selling it, giving it away, or liquidating it. Each option has significant implications for the company's financial and operational health and the owner's future.

One of the first steps in planning an exit strategy is identifying or eliminating potential buyers. Here are the types of buyers to consider:

1. Family Members

Selling to a family member often results in the lowest valuation. This option might be favored for its simplicity and the emotional comfort of keeping the business in the family, but typically, it's financially less rewarding.

2. Employees and Key Employees

These sales can be Employee Stock Ownership Plans (ESOPs) or direct sales to management. While these options keep the business in familiar hands, they typically result in a lower valuation than external buyers.

Management Buyouts (MBOs) are a common variation here. In an MBO, the existing management team purchases the business from its current owners, using a combination of personal funds, investor contributions (such as private equity firms), and debt financing. Because the management team already understands the company's operations, the transition can be smoother. Owners often consider MBOs when they believe the current management can run the company more effectively under private ownership.

Leveraged Buyouts (LBOs), in contrast, are typically led by outside buyers such as private equity firms. An LBO involves financing most of the purchase with debt, using the acquired company's assets and cash flows as collateral. The goal is often to improve operations, reduce costs, and eventually sell the company at a higher value. In LBOs, the existing management team may or may not remain in place depending on the buyer's strategy.

3. Value Buyers

Value buyers are split into two types:
Small Value Buyers—individuals or entities seeking a fair price who may require seller financing and favorable terms.
Large Value Buyers—financially capable buyers who can pay up-front, often with financing already secured.

4. Strategic Buyers

Strategic buyers may pay a premium for a business that fits perfectly with their plans, regardless of its standalone financial metrics.

Other Strategies Beyond Direct Sale

Going Public

Going public is a path typically suited for medium to larger companies with strong growth potential, established revenue streams, and scalable operations. Ideal candidates often have a large addressable market, strong brand recognition, and a capable management team experienced in executing growth strategies. Public investors also look for a clear path to profitability, a track record of operational excellence, and readiness to meet regulatory and compliance requirements. Businesses with disruptive innovation or unique intellectual property may also attract significant IPO interest.

Refinancing or Recapitalizing

Refinancing or recapitalizing can be an effective way to restructure a company's capital to meet exit goals without selling outright.

The process generally involves:

1. **Assessment** of the company's debt, equity, and cash flow.
2. **Goal setting**—for example, reducing interest expense, freeing up liquidity, or providing partial owner payout.

3. **Evaluating options**, such as renegotiating debt, securing new financing at better terms, or bringing in a new investor.
4. **Negotiation** with lenders or investors to secure favorable terms.
5. **Execution** of the restructuring.
6. **Implementation** of operational adjustments to support the new capital structure.

Benefits include improved financial flexibility, reduced interest costs, liquidity for stakeholders, and capital for growth. However, these transactions are typically more attractive in lower interest rate environments and require a skilled team—lenders, tax advisors, and cash-flow analysts—to avoid unintended consequences.

Liquidation

Liquidating—closing the business and selling its assets—is typically a last resort. It may be the right decision in cases of insolvency, persistent losses, overwhelming debt, major market decline, serious legal issues, failed turnaround efforts, or lack of viable buyers. While sometimes chosen for strategic reasons (such as exiting a declining division), liquidation should be carefully planned with legal guidance to minimize negative impacts on stakeholders and to ensure an orderly wind-down.

Exit Strategy Considerations

Family Matters

Transferring business ownership within the family brings unique challenges, particularly when multiple children are involved, which can impact the business's future and the relationships within the family. Children in family businesses often grow up with different levels of involvement and aspirations regarding the business. For example, one child might start from a grassroots level, learning every aspect of the business by starting in the warehouse and gradually working their way up. Another might acquire formal business education and external corporate experience, returning with a fresh perspective and possibly more technical business skills. This sets the stage for potential conflict regarding who is more suited to lead the business.

Another major challenge is the financial aspect of the transfer. It's common for the next generation not to have sufficient resources to buy the business outright. This often necessitates the current owner either selling the business at a significant discount or carrying the financing themselves, which can complicate the owner's retirement planning and financial security.

The lack of clear communication and preparation for the next generation is an oversight in many family business transitions. Owners often assume they know what the future leaders want or how they will want to run the business without engaging in open and honest dialogue about these topics. Studies have shown that such assumptions can lead to misaligned expectations and strategic directions. If family members have been minimally involved or sheltered from the business realities, they might be ill-prepared to take over when the time comes.

To address these issues effectively, start the planning process early and involve all potential successors in open conversations about the future of the business. This includes:

- Developing a clear succession plan that considers both the business's needs and the individual aspirations of potential successors.
- Engaging in family governance practices, such as regular meetings to discuss the business's direction and allowing everyone's voice to be heard, is beneficial.
- Professional development for all family members interested in the business, giving them the necessary skills and knowledge to succeed.
- Financial planning to ensure the business transition does not burden the exiting owner or the business's liquidity.

Selling to Shareholders

One of the main advantages of selling to current shareholders is their familiarity with the business. Having been involved with the company, whether actively or as passive investors, they possess a foundational understanding of the business's operations and strategic direction. This knowledge helps create a smooth transition, minimizing the learning curve typically associated with new ownership. Shareholders are also likely to have established relationships with key customers and understand the importance of these connections to the business's success. Leveraging these existing relationships can help maintain customer loyalty and business continuity during the transition period.

While shareholders may understand the business from an investment perspective, they might not possess the necessary management skills to run the company. This gap can lead to operational challenges if not addressed. Shareholders who have primarily been passive investors may find the day-to-day demands of business management overwhelming without the proper support and training.

Another significant challenge is the financial capability of the shareholders to buy out the business. Like family members, shareholders might not have enough personal resources to fund the purchase. This situation often necessitates creative financing solutions, such as seller financing, which can complicate the exit process and potentially delay the complete financial separation of the exiting owner from the business.

To maximize the benefits and minimize the risks of selling to other shareholders, consider implementing the following strategies:

- ➜ Providing training and development opportunities for shareholders who lack essential business management skills is crucial. This can involve formal education, mentoring, or gradual involvement in day-to-day management tasks.
- ➜ Early planning and transparent discussions about the financial aspects of the transition are essential. This might include exploring external financing options or structuring the sale to allow for gradual payment.
- ➜ A well-structured transition plan outlining each ownership change phase can help mitigate potential disruptions. This plan should include clear communication strategies, timelines, and roles and responsibilities for the exiting owner and the incoming shareholders.

Attention to these strategies maintains the legacy of your business while fostering its future growth under new ownership.

Employee Stock Ownership Plans (ESOPs)

ESOPs are a popular topic among small business owners interested in transitioning ownership. An ESOP allows a lender to loan money to the ESOP trust, which then purchases the owner's stock. This transaction turns employees into partial owners of the company. While this model can work for any size company, the setup costs make it more feasible for businesses valued at least $10 million, with $20 million being ideal under current financial conditions. The cost-effectiveness of ESOPs also fluctuates with interest rates, adding another layer of complexity.

For owners, ESOPs offer a way to ensure the continuity of the business while providing a meaningful benefit to employees. When becoming part-owners, employees typically feel more invested in the business's success, potentially leading to improved performance and morale.

One of our past clients, a highly successful construction company, was interested in transitioning to an ESOP. The owner was enthusiastic about the idea, believing it would empower his employees and secure the company's future. We advised a thorough evaluation of the management team, which would be crucial to the company's success post-transition.

After interviewing the key employees expected to lead the company, significant issues were uncovered. Departments were territorial and did not cooperate reasonably, and none of the department heads displayed the necessary leadership skills to run the company effectively. Despite these warnings, the owner proceeded with the ESOP.

Unfortunately, the company went bankrupt within a year of implementing the ESOP. The internal conflicts we identified and inadequate leadership led to the company's demise. The owner lost not only his business but also the financial security he had built. This example highlights several lessons for business owners considering an ESOP:

- **Management Team Evaluation:** Assess whether the current management team has the capability and cohesion to lead the company post-transition.
- **Understanding ESOP Dynamics**: Owners must fully understand the complexities and requirements of an ESOP, including the need for an independent trustee and possibly a board of directors.
- **Employee Readiness:** Employees must be prepared for ownership responsibilities, understanding that their investment in company stock will significantly impact their financial future.

ESOPs, while beneficial in specific contexts, are not suitable for every business. They require a solid management team, adequate financial structuring, and a deep understanding of their long-term implications. Business owners must approach this transition strategy with thorough preparation and realistic expectations to avoid potential pitfalls and ensure the longevity and health of the business.

Selling to a Third Party

While selling to a third party might be the most straightforward exit regarding transaction complexity, finding the right buyer can be difficult. The search for a third-party buyer usually requires a broader approach than selling to family members or employees. You must market the business extensively, possibly working with a business broker to reach a wider audience. Identifying a suitable buyer who can purchase the business can be a lengthy process that requires strategic planning.

Once a third-party buyer is found, the sale process can be clean. If the buyer is a larger value buyer, they likely have the necessary financing ready, allowing them to complete the purchase quickly and efficiently. This buyer may pay outright, significantly reducing the financial risks for the seller, who receives their funds immediately.

Third-party transactions often involve a transition period, during which the previous owner might be asked to stay on for a time, ranging from a few days to several years, to create a smooth handover. This can be beneficial as it provides continuity for the business and its employees.

One key consideration, especially for C corporations, is whether the sale will be structured as an asset or stock purchase. Third-party buyers often prefer asset purchases to mitigate risks, which can lead to unfavorable tax implications for the seller. In contrast, sales to family members or employees are more likely to involve stock purchases, which can be more tax-efficient for the seller.

Navigating a third-party sale requires strict confidentiality to protect the business's sensitive information. Business owners often underestimate the importance of non-disclosure agreements and properly vetting potential buyers. Employing a team of experts, including business brokers, attorneys, and financial advisors, ensures that all aspects of the sale are handled professionally, from initial marketing to final negotiations. This team approach helps to safeguard against liabilities and keeps the sale moving forward in an orderly and legal manner.

No Regrets

We've previously mentioned the well-circulated statistic that according to the Exit Planning Institute, about 70% of business owners regret selling their business within a year. This regret can often be attributed to inadequate preparation, lack of support, or failure to understand the financial and emotional aspects of the transaction entirely. Most business owners will sell a business once in their lifetime, meaning they often lack the experience that repeat buyers bring to the table. Buyers typically engage skilled advisors to perform due diligence, whether seasoned or new. Therefore, as a seller, surrounding yourself with knowledgeable professionals—lawyers, accountants, business brokers, Certified Exit Planning Advisors, and financial advisors—ensures you are equally well-prepared and advised.

We encourage you to utilize this team to fully explore your proposed exit strategy to identify potential pitfalls and unforeseen challenges. This means understanding the transaction itself and its aftereffects, including tax implications and lifestyle changes. Know what you need from the sale regarding the net proceeds required to meet your post-exit goals. Also, have a clear vision of what you want to do after exiting to guide the timing and nature of the sale, ensuring it aligns with your broader life plans. Doing so ensures that the final chapter of your business story is as rewarding as the journey that preceded it.

KEY TAKEAWAYS

- Analyze the external market and internal company dynamics to choose an exit strategy that maximizes financial gains and aligns with personal and employee considerations.

- Involve family members early in succession planning to mitigate risks associated with transferring ownership, ensuring clarity and preparation for future leaders.

- Understand the distinctions between MBOs, LBOs, ESOPs, and third-party sales to match the right strategy to your business's situation.

- When considering refinancing or recapitalization, carefully evaluate interest rate conditions, tax implications, and long-term cash flow impacts.

- Selling to a third party often necessitates extensive marketing and reliance on professional advisors to handle confidentiality and legal compliance.

- Prepare for the exit by understanding the sale's financial, emotional, and lifestyle impacts to avoid regrets and align the transition with broader life goals.

CHAPTER SEVEN
Beyond Business: Health, Retirement, and Legacy

The essence of exit planning is aligning your business, financial, and personal goals—this chapter focuses on the personal aspect, the vital third leg of the stool. Think of this as the cherry on top of your personal planning. Since 50% of business exits aren't on the owner's terms, early and thoughtful planning is essential.

In previous discussions, we've touched on a startling revelation: 70% of business owners regret their decision to sell within the first year. Why? Because the life they envisioned post-business isn't fulfilling or they haven't planned for it effectively. Imagine moving from a 60-hour workweek, where you're constantly engaged, to suddenly spending all that time at home with your spouse asking, "Are you REALLY going to be home all day?" It's a dramatic shift and not always an easy one.

When asked about their post-business plans, many business owners might respond with a nonchalant, "I'll figure it out." This attitude often leads to frustration and regret. Our goal is to take a proactive and structured approach to transition planning. It's not just about finding activities to fill your time; it's about creating a meaningful next chapter in your life.

Owning a business can be a solitary journey, and surprisingly, life after business can feel just as lonely. Don't just plan for the end of your business life but for the richness of your personal life after. We often start with an activity to help owners articulate their "personal purpose." This process begins with you writing down what matters most to you. It's best done away from the distractions of daily business operations. Our offices often serve as a retreat for business owners to step back and think deeply about their futures without the constant pull of business demands.

One of the most pivotal aspects of creating a successful exit strategy is ensuring your family is informed and involved from the outset. It used to be common for meetings to involve just the business owner or perhaps a spouse. However, this often led to complications, especially if something unexpected happened, like the owner's passing. The remaining family members would be left puzzled, questioning past decisions like, "Why did they do that?"

Bring family members into the conversation early to prevent misunderstandings and complications. Keep them informed and actively seek their input and involvement. This inclusion is crucial because once the owner is no longer in charge—whether due to retirement or passing—it becomes significantly more challenging to alter or unwind the business decisions that were made previously.

We frequently remind owners that exit planners are not mind readers. If you're contemplating or planning something, communicate that to your family and your exit planning team. About two weeks ago, we reminded an owner, "Don't assume your family knows what's happening in your head." Bringing them into your thought process and planning helps align your goals with theirs and strengthens family bonds. They'll appreciate being part of the journey, and it will bring everyone closer together.

Finding Purpose and Building a Legacy Post-Business

A significant part of finding a new purpose often involves the concept of legacy. While many entrepreneurs engage in occasional charitable acts, few have taken steps to establish a legacy that aligns with their deepest values and aspirations. This can be a profound journey, transforming mere donations into a lasting impact that embodies their life's work and passions.

Uncovering your personal purpose can be as structured as it is introspective. It begins with questions about what truly matters to you. What inspires you? What are you passionate about? What do you desire that you currently lack, and what could you live without? These questions pave the way for deeper reflection.

Once you identify these core values and desires, you can make small, consistent choices that reflect this purpose. To facilitate this, we encourage setting SMART goals—Specific, Measurable, Achievable, Relevant, and Time-bound.

The first step in clarifying these goals is to engage in open conversations with those closest to you—your family, friends, and business partners. Discussing your thoughts and intentions with your support network opens new perspectives and grounds your ideas in reality. It's one thing to have a concept in your head and quite another to articulate it and explore its feasibility with others.

Once these conversations begin, it's vital to write down your ideas. This practice helps solidify your thoughts and provides a reference to revisit and revise over time. What seems like a solid plan often loses its luster after some reflection or better ideas emerge as you discuss and dwell on your initial thoughts.

Start thinking about what comes next before your business is ready to sell. Your personal life goals should evolve in tandem with your exit planning. By starting this process early, you ensure a seamless transition where your post-business life is an extension of the careful planning that characterized your business strategy.

As you begin to align your personal purpose with your business activities, you'll likely notice a decrease in stress. This alignment helps you live more congruently, reducing the cognitive dissonance from living a life that doesn't reflect your values. Starting to make these adjustments while you are still involved in your business sets the stage for a smoother transition and a more fulfilling life post-exit.

Total Health in Exit Planning

"Total health" encompasses far more than just the absence of disease; it involves achieving a state of complete physical, mental, and social well-being. This holistic approach to health is crucial for any business owner contemplating their exit strategy.

If you neglect any aspect of your total health while running your business, you might be forced to exit earlier than planned—and likely not on your terms. An unplanned exit can have significant repercussions, not just personally but also for the continuity and legacy of your business.

When people think of health, they often consider their physical and perhaps financial health. However, total health extends beyond these aspects. The World Health Organization recognizes seven aspects of health:

1. **Physical Health:** Ensuring your body is healthy and capable.
2. **Mental Health:** Maintaining cognitive function and emotional resilience.
3. **Social Health:** Having strong, supportive relationships.
4. **Emotional Health:** Managing emotions in a way that fosters growth and stability.
5. **Intellectual Health:** Engaging in continuous learning and challenges.
6. **Environmental Health:** Living and working in healthy and stimulating environments.
7. **Occupational Health:** Gaining satisfaction and fulfillment from your work.

These dimensions of health are interlinked, and imbalance in one area can lead to stress and problems in others. For business owners, misalignment can impact personal well-being and business performance. Aligning these areas helps manage stress and maintain control over the exit process.

To effectively integrate total health into your exit planning, it is essential to consider each area and how it might be affected by the transition out of business ownership. This might involve strategic planning to enhance specific areas of health, engaging with professionals for support, or making lifestyle changes that promote well-being.

Proactive Health Management

Ensuring you are in top condition as you move into this next stage of life is imperative, not just for the success of your exit strategy but for the quality of life you aspire to afterwards.

One of the best steps is to maintain regular health check-ups. A concierge physician might be a worthwhile investment. In today's fast-paced medical environment, getting timely and meaningful time with a physician can be challenging. A concierge doctor provides personalized care, offering dedicated time and attention, which is vital as you prepare for a significant life transition.

In our comprehensive exit planning program, we recognize the importance of this aspect so strongly that by month seven, we bring in a health professional to discuss these topics with business owners. This session has become one of the top three meetings in our program, valued highly by owners who often express that no one has previously taken the time to discuss their health in the context of business transition.

Filling Your Time

Hobby Exploration

The shift from full-time business management to retirement can lead to a void that hobbies can effectively fill. For those considering taking up new activities post-business—skydiving, golf, or any other pursuit—it's wise to test these waters before committing. Diving into new hobbies during the later stages of your business career can provide a realistic preview of whether these activities will truly resonate with you once you have more time on your hands.

We approach hobbies from a process-oriented perspective, emphasizing their capacity to cover multiple aspects of total health. Engaging in a hobby can do much more than pass the time. It can significantly enhance your intellectual, social, emotional, and even spiritual well-being. Each area contributes to the total health equation, helping you maintain a balanced life after business.

Consulting and Mentorship

The transition from active management to retirement doesn't have to mean stepping away from the business world entirely. Consulting and mentorship offer powerful avenues for leveraging your accumulated expertise while continuing to make a meaningful impact.

Consulting allows you to utilize your creative abilities and deep well of knowledge to assist others, which can be rewarding. It engages various aspects of total health—occupational, by keeping you professionally active; social, by connecting you with other business professionals; emotional, by providing fulfillment; and environmental, if your consulting work takes you to new and stimulating settings. This multifaceted engagement makes consulting an attractive option for many retiring business owners who may not have extensive hobbies or other retirement plans but still crave the intellectual stimulation and personal satisfaction of their working lives.

Mentorship is another viable path that allows you to give back and forge a legacy that extends beyond your direct business achievements. By mentoring up-and-coming entrepreneurs or less experienced business owners, you impart valuable lessons that can shape industries and individual lives. This role can be incredibly satisfying, as it allows you to witness and contribute to the growth and success of others.

Numerous general and industry-specific organizations exist specifically to facilitate mentorship relationships. These organizations often seek experienced business professionals eager to share their insights and experiences. Engaging with these groups can provide a structured pathway to mentorship, allowing you to impact others meaningfully while enriching your post-business life.

Leaving a Legacy

Every business owner will leave a legacy, but the nature of that legacy—whether positive or negative—can hinge significantly on the quality of their exit planning. The consequences of inadequate planning can be severe. An example involves a business we recently started working with. The owner unexpectedly passed away without a proper succession plan in place. Despite being a third-generation business valued in the tens of millions of dollars and employing over 100 people, it imploded and closed within a year of the owner's death. This situation illustrates a harsh reality: failing to plan can lead to a legacy of collapse and failure, affecting not just your family but also the livelihoods of your employees and the community your business supports.

Legacy is connected to the culture you cultivate within your business. Every business has a culture, intentionally or not, which can influence the legacy you leave. In the past, we equated a strong company culture exclusively with positive outcomes. However, experience has taught us that culture—and, by extension, legacy—can manifest as negative if not consciously and carefully managed.

We initiate discussions about legacy early in the exit planning process. Asking business owners what kind of legacy they wish to leave can sometimes be met with silence or avoidance. It's our role to guide them in recognizing that their decisions will shape how they are remembered and what they leave behind—whether they actively think about it or not. Encouraging them to envision potential scenarios can help shift their perspective and emphasize the importance of a well-considered plan that aligns with their values and aspirations for their business's future.

Whether it's through maintaining your health, exploring hobbies, engaging in consulting or mentorship, or simply preparing your business for a smooth transition, each step you take should be aimed at crafting a legacy that lasts and a post-business life filled with purpose, health, and fulfillment. Start integrating your personal needs and goals into the daily operations of your business. When you reach the next stage, you will be healthy enough to do what you envision, minimize the possibility of regret, and do the best thing for the people around you.

KEY TAKEAWAYS

- Begin considering your post-business life early, aligning your personal, financial, and business goals to ensure a fulfilling transition.

- Engage your family in the exit planning process early to prevent misunderstandings and ensure that your business and personal plans are well understood and supported.

- Develop a clear "personal purpose" by deeply reflecting on what truly matters to you, away from the distractions of your business, to guide your actions and decisions post-exit.

- Incorporate a holistic approach to your health into your exit strategy, considering physical, mental, social, emotional, intellectual, environmental, and occupational health.

- Explore and initiate activities such as hobbies, consulting, or mentorship before retiring to ensure these pursuits align with your life after business, enhancing your overall quality of life and legacy.

CHAPTER EIGHT

Value Enhancements: Group Benefits

WITH STEVE DALINIS

H aving the right benefits package can significantly improve your bottom line by helping you attract and retain better employees. When you have a more dependable, productive team that takes fewer sick days, you'll naturally see an uptick in your company's performance.

Employee benefits are consistently one of the top concerns of business owners. They aren't just a line item on your expense report; they can be one of your company's largest expenses. When you consider salaries, paid time off, education, training, medical benefits, dental benefits, vision coverage, voluntary benefits, 401(k) plans,' and bonuses, you're looking at a significant chunk of money.

Not to mention, those costs are always on the rise. You're dealing with medical benefits, claims, rate increases, PPOs, copayments, and deductibles. And most of the time, these benefits only come into play when something goes wrong—when an employee is sick, injured, or dealing with a health crisis. So, it's rare that benefits are viewed positively by employees and employers alike.

Now, think about the other side of the coin—the positive benefits like retirement plans.

Employees cash out their retirement savings and walk away when they retire. While that's great for them, as the employer, you feel like you've just lost a part of your team. It can feel like no matter what you do, you're always on the losing end when it comes to benefits.

It's tempting to think you can solve the problem by simply upping the salaries you offer. But that strategy is easy to replicate. Your competition can just as easily bump up their base salaries, and then, suddenly, you're back to square one. Plus, employees who are attracted solely by the highest pay usually do not stick around for the long haul. If they joined your company just for the paycheck, what's stopping them from leaving when someone else offers them a dollar more an hour?

There's no silver bullet when crafting the perfect benefits package. You can't just offer one great perk and call it a day. It's more like creating a recipe—think about Kentucky Fried Chicken with its 19 secret spices. That's what makes it hard to replicate. Your benefits package should be unique and comprehensive.

The Power of a Great Benefits Program

A great benefits program contributes to the overall well-being of your employees. When you offer benefits that enhance their mental and physical health, you create a work environment where people are motivated to stay and contribute. Educated employees who can access the care they need are more likely to perform at their best, which, in turn, supports the long-term success of your business.

Of course, implementing a benefits program comes with costs. For example, medical, dental, and vision benefits typically represent a large portion of those costs. The good news is that many of these expenses are tax-deductible, which can ease the financial burden on your business. Retirement plans can even be structured to provide significant advantages for you as the employer and for your team members.

There's a common misconception that contributions to retirement plans must be equal for everyone. That's not true. You can design a retirement plan that weighs the employer's and key employees' benefits, allowing you to provide more value to those critical to your business's success. The same flexibility applies to medical benefits. You can offer different plans to everyone. You can tailor richer benefits packages for the employees you want to retain the most.

Incentive-based compensation is another powerful tool within a benefits package. When designed correctly, these incentives can drive growth and profitability. For example, you can structure compensation so that key employees—those directly contributing to the company's success—receive substantial pay increases funded by the new revenue they help generate. This approach aligns your employees' interests with the company's growth.

Balancing Costs for Employers and Employees

When we build a benefits package, we consider three factors: the employer's cost, the employee's cost, and, most importantly, the employee's cost to access care. If your average employee can't afford to see a doctor, you and your employees are wasting money on a plan that doesn't work. It's essential to create a three-pronged balance where the business owner's expenses are justified, the employees are supported, and the employees can actually afford to use the benefits you provide.

The Evolution of Employee Benefits

If you look back 30 years, employee benefits were much simpler. It was mostly about providing basic medical, dental, and vision coverage back then. The costs were more reasonable, and the plans were straightforward. However, as time has passed, the range of available benefits has expanded significantly, and the designs of these plans have become more complex. This evolution means that today, you can customize benefits to suit your company's and employee groups' specific needs. With this increased complexity comes increased costs, so finding ways to manage and lower these costs is more important than ever.

Today, healthcare remains the most valued benefit among employees. However, there has been a notable shift in healthcare delivery, primarily driven by changes like the Affordable Care Act (ACA). One major change is the move from Health Maintenance Organizations (HMOs) to Preferred Provider Organizations (PPOs), which allow employees to receive care without needing referrals, giving them more flexibility in choosing their healthcare providers.

There's also been a growing appreciation for chamber plans, which can offer tremendous savings for employees while improving their access to care. Beyond healthcare, benefits like dental, vision, and long-term disability are equally important. Adding Health Savings Accounts (HSAs) and Flexible Spending Accounts (FSAs) can also provide pre-tax savings for employees, making these options highly valued.

Another trend we see today is employees desiring multiple choices within their benefits plans. Offering a plan that includes several different options—such as HMO, PPO, and others—allows people to choose the plan that best fits their needs and budget. This flexibility is necessary because it empowers employees to decide about their own healthcare based on what is most affordable and beneficial.

Benefits Advantages

One advantage of offering a comprehensive benefits program is the tax implications, both for the employer and the employees. Most of these benefits are tax deductible for employers, which can significantly reduce the overall tax burden. On the other hand, employees generally receive these benefits tax-free, making them even more valuable.

It's important to ensure that the portion of healthcare costs paid by employees is done on a pre-tax basis. This approach lowers the tax bill for both the employer and the employees. For instance, with retirement plan contributions, employers can take a dollar-for-dollar tax deduction while still retaining 100% of that contribution for themselves. This is one of the few areas where you can fully benefit from the tax deduction and still keep your money.

Section 125 plans are another critical tool in managing the tax implications of employee benefits. These plans allow you to pre-tax your employees' share of premiums, covering various benefits such as additional accident insurance, life insurance, and vision coverage. When these benefits are offered pre-tax, employees save on their taxable income, and employers see a reduction in payroll taxes.

Section 125 plans save money on FICA and FUTA taxes and reduce the employees' taxable gross income, meaning they are paying for their benefits with tax-free dollars. Numerous other federally approved plans allow employees to pay for certain expenses with pre-tax dollars. Working with a Third Party Administrator (TPA) to manage these deductions can streamline the process, helping everyone access their benefits conveniently, often through their own individual card.

For larger groups, these tax savings can be substantial enough to enable the employer to increase their contributions to employee benefits. This creates a win-win situation: the employer saves on taxes, and employees receive more comprehensive benefits while reducing their taxable income.

Customization

Regarding employee benefits, one size definitely does not fit all. You can customize your benefits offerings to meet the specific needs of your workforce, but it's crucial to ensure they are cohesive and don't overlap in ways that could lead to inefficiencies or unnecessary costs.

For example, you might have a health insurance plan with specific deductibles and copayments. If you introduce a voluntary benefit product to help cover those costs, but it aligns differently from your existing health plan, you're not maximizing the value of those benefits. Similarly, if you have a sick leave policy and add a disability plan that overlaps it, you could double-pay for the same coverage. Customization is key, but you need proper integration to ensure your benefits package is comprehensive and cost-effective.

Customization has become more important now than ever, especially with the need for electronic enrollment options. Employees should be able to obtain their enrollment materials easily and have 24/7 access to information about their health plans. This is especially crucial for those moments when they have a question in the middle of the night or need to review their benefits quickly.

For mid-sized and larger groups, customization involves tailoring options to meet the diverse needs of different segments within the workforce. Whether dealing with blue-collar, gray-collar, or white-collar workers, each group may have different priorities and requirements. Offering multiple medical plans, sometimes up to six different options, allows you to cater to the varied circumstances of your employees.

One area that has become increasingly critical is mental health. In many ways, mental health is just as important, if not more so, than physical health. Mental health support should be a top priority when customizing benefits packages today. This includes implementing employee assistance programs, promoting physical wellness through annual check-ups, and ensuring employees can access the mental health resources they need.

In the past, benefits discussions focused heavily on things like HMOs, copays, and deductibles. But today, the conversation has shifted. When we conduct benefits meetings now, we spend about 70% of the time educating employees on how to access care, emphasizing mental and physical well-being. The old days of focusing solely on the financial aspects of healthcare are gone. Now, it's about customizing a benefits package that truly supports the holistic health of your employees.

Measuring the Effectiveness of Your Benefits Program

To truly understand the value and impact of your benefits program, it's essential to track specific metrics and indicators that reveal how well your offerings work for your business and your employees.

- **Tax Savings:** The first and most straightforward metric is the tax savings that your benefits program generates. Offering these benefits can reduce your overall tax burden compared to not having a benefits program in place. This is a tangible, immediate way to see the financial effectiveness of your benefits offerings.

- **Productivity:** If you notice increased productivity after implementing or improving your benefits program, that's a good sign your decision is paying off. Alongside productivity, tracking sick time, job-related injuries, and absenteeism can provide insight into the health and well-being of your workforce. For example, offering short-term and long-term disability coverage can reduce employees falsely claiming work-related injuries, saving your business significant money in workers' compensation claims.

- **Utilization:** Utilization metrics are also critical. Are your employees using their benefits effectively? Are they choosing the appropriate levels of care, such as opting for urgent care over emergency room visits when appropriate? The answers to these questions help assess whether your employees are making the most of their benefits and whether those benefits are reducing overall healthcare costs.

One of the best ways to gauge the effectiveness of your benefits program is by working with a high-quality health broker who has your best interests at heart. Unlike an insurance company agent, a broker represents you, the employer. Their fiduciary responsibility is to ensure that the plan they design offers the best value for your company and your employees. A knowledgeable broker knows how to integrate multiple benefit packages to enhance the overall value, ensuring that the benefits not only compete in the marketplace but also meet the specific needs of your employees.

A quality broker stays in contact with your employee group throughout the year. Regular communication helps build a relationship between the broker and your employees, making it easier for them to navigate any claims or issues that arise.

When securing the best benefits for your business, especially in the smaller group market, it's important to understand how rates work. Generally, if the census, benefit design, and quote date are the same, the health insurance or other benefits rates will be the same, regardless of the broker. However, some brokers might tweak certain details to make it seem like they are offering a better deal. The reality is that once you implement the plan, the rate is the rate, no matter who your broker is.

For groups with more than 50 employees, utilization data becomes valuable. A good broker can track where your healthcare dollars are going—whether it's urgent care, prescriptions, physical therapy, or mental health services. This information is imperative when it comes to renewal time. By understanding these patterns, you can make informed decisions about adjusting copays or plan features to drive better health outcomes and stabilize costs.

Finally, larger groups should consider forming an internal benefits committee. These committees can gather employee feedback and report back to the business owner. This allows for a more grassroots understanding of how the workforce perceives and uses the benefits program. A good health broker should support this process, helping to facilitate communication and ensure that the program remains aligned with your team's requirements.

As a business owner, your responsibility is to your employees and your company's future. Work with the right broker to provide a benefits program that supports your employees' well-being, enhances productivity, and secures your business's financial health. Remember, the right benefits package isn't just a cost—it's an investment in your company's most valuable asset: your people.

KEY TAKEAWAYS

- Employee benefits require a unique and comprehensive package to attract and retain top talent, thereby enhancing the value of your business.

- A strong benefits program boosts productivity, reduces absenteeism, and supports long-term business success.

- Customizing and integrating benefits, especially mental health and flexible options, maximizes their value.

- Tax strategies like Section 125 plans can reduce costs for both employers and employees.

- Partnering with a knowledgeable broker ensures your benefits package aligns with your business goals and employee needs.

CHAPTER NINE
Putting It All Together

O ver the past 35 plus years, we've seen business owners receive a hefty report full of recommendations or suggestions, but they are left to implement it all on their own. This is challenging for a couple of reasons.

It is likely the first time these owners are navigating something like this, so it's uncharted territory. It can be overwhelming to figure out how to implement such a comprehensive plan. Second, and even more importantly, business owners already work 40, 60, or even 80 hours a week. Adding the responsibility of implementing a complex plan on top of that is almost impossible. As a result, many owners end up shelving the report, thinking they'll get to it when things slow down. But, as we all know, things rarely slow down.

That's why having an independent outside person or team is critical to help implement the plan. One thing that sets us apart is not just delivering the overall strategy and plan but also working with the business owners, key people, and family members to ensure everything gets done.

Value Assessment

We've talked extensively about the three legs of the stool: personal, financial, and business. Specifically, the Strategic Coach plays a pivotal role in the business aspect. It all starts with an assessment to evaluate where value lies within the business.

In the past, wealth was primarily seen as physical assets like property, plant, and equipment. However, technology has disrupted this system. Today, wealth is created through our ability to work with intangible assets, also known as knowledge assets. Managing these intellectual assets has become essential for businesses, although many owners may not have considered this perspective before.

Understanding and utilizing intangible assets can significantly increase a business's value. Regular feedback from a professional about these assets and how they are being used can amplify the valuation multiple. Leveraging these intangible assets requires a team and a process. This team will also assess structure, human capital, customer relations, and competition.

Addressing Low-Scoring Areas

Typically, we prioritize the areas that score the lowest in these assessments. This approach ensures we address the most critical issues, establishing a solid foundation for a successful succession plan. One of the most common areas that often requires attention is related to employees. You must have the right people prepared to carry out the necessary tasks.

Another frequent focus is on the business's structure and systems. Ensuring that these are well-organized and efficient is essential for smooth operations and can significantly impact the overall value of your business. It's important to note that the specific priorities will vary based on the unique findings of your assessment.

Strategic vs. Operational Plans

A misconception among business owners is that they equate their day-to-day operations with a strategic plan. Typically, an operational plan focuses on the immediate or short-term activities within the business, managing what's happening daily, like everyone knowing their roles and responsibilities. However, this differs from a strategic plan, especially a strategic exit plan.

A strategic plan is much more long-term, looking out several years into the future. It focuses on the vision of where you want to take the business and how to get there. But a vision alone isn't enough.

To execute a strategic exit plan effectively, we focus on vision, team, and commitment.

- **Vision**: This is the foundation of the strategic exit plan. It provides a clear picture of where the business is headed and the objectives it aims to achieve.

- **Team**: Having a capable team is equally important. This team includes the internal staff, external advisors, and professionals who bring expertise in various areas, such as financial planning, legal considerations, and market analysis.

- **Commitment**: Finally, a strong commitment must be made to implement the plan. This means regularly reviewing and adjusting the plan to adapt to changing circumstances. It's not enough to set a plan in motion and forget about it; ongoing management and flexibility are key to its success.

The Role of 90-Day Sprints in Exit Planning

One of the most effective strategies in exit planning is using 90-day sprints. These are not just quick fixes but carefully designed to tackle larger, potentially complex projects specific to the business's unique situation. While certain foundational elements, like having all the governing documents in place, are standard across businesses, the real value comes from addressing each business's unique challenges and opportunities.

You might wonder, "How do you eat an elephant?" The answer is, of course, "One bite at a time." This saying encapsulates the idea behind 90-day sprints. These sprints break down the work into manageable, achievable sections. When you have a vision for your business's future, countless tasks must be completed, often taking time.

Ninety-day sprints are structured to create momentum and drive toward a successful outcome within a short timeframe. The first sprint sets the tone for the entire process. It helps identify what needs to be done, who is responsible, and the timeline for completion. This initial sprint is about building a rhythm, a concept often discussed in industry circles. Establishing this rhythm is essential for the plan's ongoing success.

Our approach often involves a 12-month program that addresses all aspects of personal and financial planning, culminating in focusing on the business itself. By months eight and nine, we're crafting a strategic plan, and the first 90-day sprint marks the conclusion of this first year.

Plan A, Plan B, and Plan C in a Flexible Exit Strategy

You might think that everything is set in stone once you have a plan. However, as a business owner, you know that things rarely go exactly as planned. Business environments evolve, and what works today may not be viable tomorrow. That's why you must have a flexible exit strategy that includes multiple options, often called Plan A, B, and C.

Plan A: The Ideal Scenario

Plan A is defined as the most desirable path for your exit. This is the plan where everything aligns perfectly, meeting your most important goals. For example, Plan A might involve achieving a specific financial target to bridge a wealth gap, fulfilling a family legacy objective, or transitioning ownership to key employees. This plan is based on the best-case scenario, assuming market conditions and internal business factors remain favorable.

Plan B and Plan C: Contingency Plans

We can't always predict the future. That's where Plan B and Plan C come into play. These contingency plans provide alternative paths if Plan A doesn't work out. Plan B might be the next best option, though it may not be as ideal. It serves as a fallback in case unexpected circumstances—like market downturns, changes in buyer interest, or unforeseen challenges—arise.

Plan C, if necessary, offers yet another alternative. While these backup plans might not be as desirable as Plan A, they are crucial for maintaining momentum and avoiding setbacks. The goal is to ensure you are not forced into a quick, unplanned decision that could negatively impact your exit.

To prepare for these possibilities, we conduct advanced hypothetical scenario analysis. This helps us understand the potential outcomes of different plans and ensures that we are ready for various situations. By having these plans in place, you are prepared for the best-case scenario and equipped to handle less favorable conditions.

The Execution Challenge:
The Role of a Strategic Coach

As we discussed earlier, the Master Planning process can have many moving parts, including coordination with various stakeholders like attorneys, CPAs, benefits advisors, family members, and key employees. A skilled Strategic Coach can manage these relationships and ensure everything runs smoothly.

The coach's job is to minimize the impact on the business's day-to-day operations, allowing the owner and team to maintain their regular routines while developing and implementing the Master Planning strategies. A major part of this role is keeping everyone on task and on schedule and ensuring that the agreed-upon timeline is adhered to.

In many ways, the Strategic Coach is like a sports coach. We often compare ourselves to quarterbacks, but the Strategic Coach's role is broader. They design the playbook, call the plays, and evaluate performance. They are responsible for making adjustments based on feedback, delegating tasks, and managing accountability.

Preparing for an exit is like playing a game, with the actual exit representing the final quarter or the last three minutes. There's a lot that leads up to this point. Just as a coach would do during a game, the Strategic Coach helps the business owner and their team pivot as needed, depending on the challenges and opportunities that arise. This involves constantly adjusting internal and external factors to align the business with its strategic goals.

One significant benefit of having a Strategic Coach is the fresh perspective they bring to the business. When running your business for a long time, it's easy to overlook specific issues or take certain aspects for granted. A Strategic Coach, CPAs, and other advisors can provide invaluable insights by spending time on-site, reviewing financials, and assessing operations. This often uncovers potential red flags that could be concerning to a buyer.

There's a saying, "Go ugly early," which means being upfront about any potential issues in a sales process. A Strategic Coach can help you position and explain these issues, setting the narrative to present your company in the best possible light. This transparency can be crucial in securing a deal, preventing future surprises that could derail negotiations.

Working with a Strategic Coach can make implementing the Master Planning strategies feel seamless, almost like a non-event. The coach integrates the plan into day-to-day operations without disrupting the business. Regular reviews and progress measurements are essential components of this process, providing tangible evidence of the strides being made.

Business owners are often pleasantly surprised during these reviews to see how much progress has been made. This structured approach keeps everyone accountable, helps maintain momentum, and helps focus on long-term goals. The success of this process is evident compared to businesses that attempt to execute an exit deal without guidance.

We've seen numerous businesses that chose to handle the exit transaction on their own without the guidance of a Strategic Coach. Unfortunately, the vast majority of these cases do not end well. A particularly memorable example involves a successful multi-generational business worth an estimated $40-50 million. After the original owner passed away, the next generation decided to proceed without external guidance, believing they could manage everything themselves. Within a year, the business imploded, resulting in a fire sale that promptly ended the company's legacy.

"The kids running it into the ground" has become the new family legacy, replacing a once-successful, three-generation enterprise. Honestly, they could have won an award for running a booming business into the ground faster than we have ever seen. This case highlights the importance of having expert guidance during the transition period. A Strategic Coach provides a structured approach and fresh insights while helping to mitigate risks that could otherwise lead to disastrous outcomes.

Overcoming Challenges

A big hurdle business owners face when transitioning from planning to execution is related to human capital—their employees. Often, it's not until you start implementing the plan that you discover who is truly capable and willing to get the work done. This phase can reveal competencies or the lack thereof, as people are held accountable for specific tasks. This realization can be surprising, especially if these individuals seemed competent during the planning phase. Spend time determining if you have the right team and whether key people are fully engaged or merely along for the ride.

Often, this process results in changes within the team. We aim to have the "right butts in the right seats," meaning that we may need to reposition people within the organization or, in some cases, let them go. This restructuring can be challenging but is often necessary to align the team with the business's strategic goals.

Another challenge is overcoming procrastination and the natural tendency to take the path of least resistance. When a business owner attempts to implement the plan alone, delaying or avoiding challenging tasks is easy. Working with a team throughout the design and execution phases helps maintain momentum. The camaraderie and the shared goal of transforming the business provide motivation and accountability. When the entire team is involved, there's a collective drive to see the project through to completion.

Moving Beyond the Plan

To maintain momentum during the execution phase, we recommend shifting the mindset around planning. In the past, we might have delivered a financial plan to a client, and the client would leave with a sense of completion, thinking the process was done. However, providing the plan is just the beginning. The next step is the strategy meeting, where we start implementing the plan.

This approach is like turning the page to the next chapter in a book. Completing the plan isn't the end; it's just one step in a series of ongoing actions. Maintaining momentum means understanding that each step leads to the next, and there's always more work to be done.

Transitioning out of your business is a unique challenge that requires a different set of skills and knowledge than running it. One of the most important pieces of advice we can offer is don't do it alone. A team of experts can help you communicate your business's value effectively, identify the right buyers or transition methods, and navigate the complexities of the exit process.

Our mission is to educate, empower, and support businesses. Education is the foundation of a great exit strategy. Be open to advice, use the resources available to you, including a knowledgeable team, and prioritize education throughout the journey. This way, you can confidently embrace the transition and achieve the best possible outcome for yourself and your business.

KEY TAKEAWAYS

- Implementing an exit plan requires more than just a report; it needs active involvement and guidance to ensure business owners don't get overwhelmed or shelve the plan.

- Focusing on intangible assets like intellectual property can significantly increase a business's value, but to fully leverage these assets, regular professional feedback is necessary.

- A comprehensive exit strategy includes a long-term strategic plan, a capable team, and a strong commitment to executing the plan while being flexible to adapt to changing circumstances.

- 90-day sprints help break down complex tasks into manageable phases, creating momentum and ensuring steady progress toward the exit plan.

- Having multiple plans (Plans A, B, C) prepares business owners for various outcomes, providing flexibility and resilience in the face of unexpected changes in the business environment.

EPILOGUE

"Access to information is not the same
as knowledge and experience."
- Hawley H. MacLean

We've shared a lot of valuable insights throughout this book—strategies, frameworks, stories, and steps to help you successfully transition your business. But if there's one thing we want to leave you with, it's this: information alone isn't enough. You need a trusted team—one that brings not just technical knowledge, but the wisdom of experience—to help you translate this information into action. That's where transformation begins.

We want to take a moment to congratulate you. You've done something most small- to mid-sized business owners never get around to: you started thinking about your transition before it's too late. Many owners wait until they're forced to react to a health issue, family crisis, or market change. But by picking up this book and reading it all the way through, you've made a proactive choice. You're choosing peace of mind over panic. You're choosing clarity, intention, and a lasting legacy. You've also chosen to prioritize your family, your team, and your future.

It may still feel like a daunting task—creating a contingency plan, a transition plan, an estate plan, and a financial plan that works for both your business and your family. But you've already begun. The fact that you've taken the time to learn, reflect, and prepare yourself mentally puts you ahead of the curve. Understanding the principles is the first step. Now it's about building your team—starting with the right leader to guide you through this process.

Procrastination is a dangerous pitfall. Owners delay because they don't have all the answers—or they don't even know what questions to ask. In our combined decades of experience, we've seen thriving businesses crumble overnight because the owner didn't have a plan when one of the Six Ds—death, disability, divorce, disagreement, distress or decline in health—struck. We've seen families lose everything, employees left jobless, and customers left hanging. These weren't bad businesses. They were just unprepared.

Please, don't let that be your story.

Start by completing our online assessment quiz. It's quick, confidential, and will provide us with a snapshot of your current situation. From there, we'll meet for a consultation to review your results and develop a plan tailored to your goals, timeline, and definition of success.

This doesn't need to be overwhelming. In fact, our entire approach is about creating the path of least resistance—for you and your business.

Step 1: Gather & Review

We'll review your assessment results, discuss your goals, and outline the documents we require from you.

Step 2: Agree & Onboard

We'll walk you through our fee structure, which typically starts with an onboarding fee and transitions to a monthly retainer.

Step 3: Plan & Implement

We'll meet regularly (usually 2–3 hours a month), with additional calls and support as needed. Over the next 6–12 months, we'll develop, implement, and communicate your plan with all stakeholders. Then, we'll set up a rhythm to monitor and refine the plan going forward.

We've seen this process change people's lives. Some owners come in uncertain, worried that their business might not be enough to meet their financial goals. But through the process, they gain clarity. They see exactly what's needed and how to get there.

Others are relieved to discover that they're already on track. They feel empowered to move forward with confidence and peace of mind.

And then some rediscover their love for the business. With stronger systems, clearer goals, and a team aligned around the future, they decide to hold onto the company a bit longer—not because they have to, but because they're having fun again.

Whatever the outcome, you'll come out of this process stronger. You'll know where you're going, how you'll get there, and who's going to help along the way.

How prepared are you for a business transition?

Take our readiness quiz to find out:

Congratulations! By reading this book, you've already taken the first step towards taking charge of your future and your business. We want to help you! Call us at 775-329-3041 or check out our website at www.macleanfinancialgroup.com.

WORKS CITED

Exit Planning Institute. (2023). *Owner readiness: What it is & why should you care?* Exit Planning Institute. Retrieved September 21, 2025, from https://blog.exit-planning-institute.org/what-is-owner-readiness Exit Planning Institute Blog

Exit Planning Institute. (2016). *Walking to destiny: 11 actions an owner must take to rapidly grow value & unlock wealth.* Independence, OH: Author.

Massachusetts Mutual Life Insurance Company & LRW. (2022). *2022 Business Owner Perspectives Study: Insights from America's Economic Engine.* https://www.massmutual.com/global/media/shared/doc/sb1020_2022.pdf

Mysogland, E. (2018, April 1). *Emotional considerations for transitions.* Exit Planning Institute. Retrieved September 21, 2025, from https://blog.exit-planning-institute.org/emotional-considerations -transitions

ABOUT HAWLEY MACLEAN

In 1990, Hawley founded MacLean Financial Group with a singular mission: to help clients promote and protect their financial freedom for a net positive plan through all of life's transitions.

His family's legacy in multi-generational wealth management spans over 150 years, deeply rooted in a tradition of financial steward-ship and client-focused service.

As President and CEO of the firm, Hawley is committed to assisting clients achieve their financial goals, transition their business successfully, and safeguard and preserve their wealth. He crafts strategies tailored to clients' unique circumstances and objectives by employing a needs-based approach to financial planning. With a clear focus on the long term, he aims to inspire confidence across all chapters of his clients' lives: today, tomorrow, and for years to come.

A dynamic leader in the financial sector, Hawley is also a founder and active director of Heritage Bank of Nevada. His contributions to the community have earned him accolades, including being named the American Heart Association's 2004 Man of the Year. As a Life Member of the Million Dollar Round Table, he showcases his dedication to professional excellence and ethical practice. Beyond the boardroom, Hawley was the driving force behind Water & Rails, Northern Nevada's largest fundraiser for ALS of Nevada. His remarkable service to the cause has been recognized with the Steve Rigazio Voice of Courage Award.

Hawley currently serves on the University of Nevada Reno College of Science Advisory Council. He has held a variety of Board roles, including: Vice-Chair Reno Tahoe Winter Games Coalition, USA Curling, Executive Board Member World Union of Olympic Cities (Lausanne, Switzerland), and the California State Railroad Museum Foundation.

When he steps away from his professional responsibilities, Hawley finds joy in traveling with his family, skiing down picturesque slopes, live steam engines, and Garden Model Railroads. His multifaceted life illustrates his commitment not just to his clients but to his community and family, making him a true steward of financial freedom and personal fulfillment.

ABOUT DAN SPRINGER

Dan is the Director of the Wealth Planning Team at MacLean Financial Group, where he is deeply committed to helping clients optimize their financial strategies for a more fulfilling life. With a diverse clientele encompassing business owners, families, and individuals, Dan recognizes the profound impact of financial decisions on present well-being and the legacy we leave behind.

Drawing on his extensive background in banking, Dan has fostered deep-rooted connections with local businesses and investment partners. For the past twenty years, he has been instrumental in helping clients navigate the intricate landscape of finance.

A true innovator in his field, Dan has developed a customized, proprietary approach to exit planning for business owners. Through meticulous analysis and tailored strategies, he ensures entrepreneurs seamlessly transition their businesses while safeguarding wealth and legacy for future generations.

Outside of his professional endeavors, Dan is driven by a passion for creating positive change in his community. Inspired by his eldest daughter, Joy, who experiences severe autism, Dan founded Joyride, a non-profit organization dedicated to providing recreational opportunities for individuals with Autism Spectrum Disorders and other disabilities.

When he's not in the office, Dan can be found immersed in outdoor adventures such as mountain biking, kayaking, hiking, snowboarding, skiing, or fishing. His unwavering belief in the importance of work-life balance underscores his commitment to delivering unparalleled service and ensuring his clients achieve the highest quality of life possible.

WHAT HAWLEY AND DAN'S CLIENTS ARE SAYING...

"In working with Maclean Financial Group, the best exercises for us were:

1. *Establishing how much monthly revenue we needed for our current lifestyle and bills, and what we wanted during retirement.*

2. *Mapping out our current expenses (budgeting) which led us to a reasonable 'per-month-investment-return-goal' for our retirement.*

3. *Once we established that reasonable monthly income number, we were able to study, quantify, and record not only our current investment strategy and returns, but to begin to plan additional revenue streams.*

4. *Establishing the dollar amount required from our business sale to meet our per-month-investment-return-goal.*

5. *My favorite...looking at the different methods of Business Sales, Business Valuation, EBITDA and Multipliers, tax consequences and strategies.*

This process let me believe that we didn't have to keep working ourselves to death in order to achieve our retirement goals. It let me understand how we could meet our monthly return goals without selling our company for huge money. It let me understand that we could maintain our current lifestyle comfortably, and in fact, even enhance it. It made me realize that most of our sacrifices were in fact, worth it.

No regrets, and I will push friends and family to get Wealth Planning from MFG...even when they think they can't afford it...because they need to afford it."

- Alby Redick

—

"We use MFG's Group Benefits, Financial Planning, and Succession Planning programs. All of which have helped me grow my company to the size it is now. We currently employ 60 people."

- Dean Maga, Owner and President of Freeport Freight Systems

www.ingramcontent.com/pod-product-compliance
Lightning Source LLC
Chambersburg PA
CBHW070933210326
41520CB00021B/6923